ESSENTIALLY
SPEAKING

A PRACTICAL GUIDE TO UNDERSTANDING THE BEST PRACTICES OF PUBLIC SPEAKING

Amanda Gilliland

Kendall Hunt
publishing company

Cover image © Shutterstock, Inc.

Kendall Hunt
publishing company

www.kendallhunt.com
Send all inquiries to:
4050 Westmark Drive
Dubuque, IA 52004-1840

Copyright © 2021 by Kendall Hunt Publishing Company

ISBN 978-1-7924-5783-8

Published in the United States of America

How important are speeches? I don't know ask the Gettysburg Address.
Oh, it didn't answer your call? Maybe because it was in the Smithsonian.
—Leslie Knope, Parks and Recreation

To all the people who think they can't speak publicly.
You are wrong and you are capable.
I believe in you.
—Mrs. G.

Contents

Acknowledgements

A lot goes into writing a book… that's why I have avoided it like the plague. Until one random day, I opened my email to find a request for writing a text book from Kendall Hunt. The rest is history and I'm so grateful to the Kendall Hunt Team for their patience and encouragement through the process.

To my Husband, Brett, your enthusiasm and encouragement have kept me going on this project. Thank you for always being the best student that I have ever had, even though you've never officially signed up for my instruction. Watching you put public speaking into practice in so many different settings and for different purposes all while having a front row seat has encouraged me that the work I do is important, even if some of the students I teach don't realize it.

To my kids, Rece and Ella, thank you for letting me torture you by correcting your phrasing and forcing you to rehearse any and all presentations you have for school. I hope one day, you will look back fondly on working together with me!

To Katie Burrall who constantly encouraged me by saying, "you got this!" over and over again, thank you for letting me use your story to encourage others and always listening when I eagerly tried to coach you through every speaking experience you've had over the last few years!

Lastly, to my colleagues in the Integrated Marketing Communications program at The University of West Alabama, thank you for your encouragement and excitement over this project. Thank you for the feedback and the requests for the book title so you can use it in your classes. Thank you for the life lessons you have shared that I may have built into my examples in class and in turned into this book. Thank you for offering advice and guidance that I could use to enhance the words on the page. Amy, Greg, Brandon, Caleb, and Tina you all have pushed me and motivated me in so many ways over the years of working together and I think that has led to this project actually getting started and ultimately finished. Please forgive me for becoming an introverted hermit during the process!

To all my students at UWA, I am so thankful that I have had the pleasure of learning from you and hearing your voices. You have inspired my words and I am forever grateful for the privilege of teaching you. YOU are capable and do not ever forget that.

—Mrs. G.

What is a Presentation?

"Speech is power: speech is to persuade, to convert, to compel."

—Ralph Waldo Emerson

Merriam-Webster Dictionary offers this definition of **presentation:** *Something set forth for the attention of the mind* (2020). What a beautiful way to think of a presentation. A presenter takes information, organizes it in a way that the minds of the audience will not only be attentive to, but they will be able to learn something, be inspired, be entertained, or even be challenged into a new way of thinking! (Fig 1.1).

© By Rido/Shutterstock.com

Fig 1.1 Presentations can look unique, whether in an auditorium or in a conference room a presentation can and should make an impact.

Source: https://www.shutterstock.com/image-photo/company-executive-presenting-new-management-strategy-1620889693

Presentation skills are not only achievable but also necessary to perform and achieve success in any situation: school, work, and personal matters. No matter the subject, a classroom setting calls for oral presentations, communication and questions with professors, and discussions with classmates. Strong verbal and written communication skills will most often be listed in desired skills for a job listing and are necessary to train fellow employees, provide customer service, and problem solve. Being able to communicate effectively and efficiently is not only important but also necessary in your personal life to clarify your needs or explain your actions be it with a place of business or an issue at a child's school. No matter the scenario, no matter the job, you will always need to have the ability to organize thoughts and communicate them in a way that captures the "attention of the mind" within the audience.

Elements of a Presentation

What are the necessary elements of a presentation? Aside from the presenter, there are several elements to consider prior to crafting your presentation: the *Audience*, the *Message*, the *Method*, and the *Setting*. If all of these elements are not considered prior to preparing a presentation, there could be a failure to achieve the goals intended with the presentation. Evaluating key factors of each element of the presentation will help the speaker achieve success with the presentation.

The Presenter is the person delivering a speech or the presentation. The Presenter should always consider how their knowledge and expertise, as well as their passions, can be dynamically delivered in order to meet the expectations of all the other elements of a presentation.

The Message is the overall concept of the presentation. A message is a communication provided to a recipient, often communicating a significant point addressing social, political, or moral themes (Oxford Languages, 2020). The presentation message takes a theme and delivers the overall importance of that theme to the listeners. The message should communicate a subject and provide value to the audience while it remains rooted in the passion and interest of the presenter.

The Audience is arguably the most important element that should be considered when crafting a presentation. The audience is the group of listeners that will hear the presentation. Approaching the process of building a presentation with the mindset of "why should my audience care?" will ensure that the message will resonate with the listeners. Without an audience, a speaker is merely talking to themselves. Without an audience there is no message because, as stated earlier, a message requires a recipient, and in this case, that recipient is the audience.

The Method is the overall way a speech is delivered. The method combines different factors to become a unique format for delivering a presentation. Many elements can shape a presenter's method making each presentation look different from the last. The type of presentation aids created, the setting for the presentation, the delivery style, the time of day, and many more factors combine to create a unique method for speaking each time a presentation is crafted.

This book is designed to give you hands-on experience in crafting, rehearsing, and delivering your presentation. Rather than thinking of this as a textbook, it should be seen as a guidebook. Much like one you would use to plan a trip. The best guidebooks on travel do not merely give details about the place you are visiting, they share the best places to tour based on interests, best restaurants to patron, and even provide you with sample itineraries based on the length of your trip or type of adventure you wish to take. In the same way, the hope for this book is that you use it as a guide for the best ways to organize your presentation, share your passions and values, communicate concepts, and deliver your speech in a dynamic and effective manner. Your journey to more effective presentation skills will still be unique to you as you will be given opportunities to use your creative ideas to make mock presentations, build elements of a speech, practice different styles of outlines, and many other activities based on the concepts in each chapter. Set specific goals for yourself as you begin to work through the challenges that are specific to you when it comes to presenting. At the end of your travels through these ideas, your goal of becoming a better presenter should be realized. Whether you simply need the confidence to stand in front of people, avoid panic when assigned a speech, be able to better organize ideas, or need to know how to deliver a speech dynamically in a way that it impacts the audience, you will find at the end of this journey that you have improved in ways that will become a foundation upon which you continue to build and develop skills with each new presentation you deliver (Fig. 1.2).

© By Ivan Kruk/Shutterstock.com

Fig 1.2 Take steps to join in each activity at the end of the chapter to practice the tips you learn.

Source: https://www.shutterstock.com/image-photo/female-hands-pen-writing-on-notebook-275161592

TAKE ACTION

1. Take a moment to reflect on your presentation ability level. On a scale from 1 to 10 with 1 being least experienced and 10 being expert level, how confident are you in your abilities as a presenter? Circle your answer:

    1   2   3   4   5   6   7   8   9   10

2. In this chapter, you were challenged to consider goals you have when it comes to presenting. Below list three top goals that you hope to achieve by the end of this book:

    _____

    _____

    _____

3. Reflect on your current daily life, what areas/activities of yours could benefit from strong communication skills? List two or three areas:

    _____

    _____

    _____

4. List three specific action steps you can take right now to begin improving and implementing your communication skills:

    _____

    _____

    _____

2 Nervousness

> **"There are only two types of speakers in the world. 1, The nervous and 2, Liars."**
>
> *—Anonymous*

This quote perfectly summarizes the population when it calls attention to nerves when speaking. Everyone gets nervous, and public speaking anxiety and nervousness are real. While nerves can be a common denominator among speakers, the response to the nervousness we all may experience can present itself in many various physiological responses at varying degrees of intensity.

Comedian Jerry Seinfeld perfectly sums up how much people fear public speaking when he said, "According to most studies, people's number one fear is public speaking. Number two is death. Death is number two. Does that sound right? This means to the average person, if you go to a funeral, you're better off in the casket than delivering the eulogy." Let's work on changing this concept by addressing our nervousness.

It is important to prepare for nerves in an upcoming presentation *by identifying and managing symptoms of public speaking anxiety, using physical and vocal mechanics to release nervous energy, and setting realistic goals for the presentation.* In this chapter you will walk through these steps in order to feel more confident about doing a presentation even in the face of any nerves or anxiety you may need to manage.

Identifying and Managing Symptoms of Public Speaking Anxiety

The first step to addressing nervousness is to evaluate what symptoms you experience when you present. While every person responds to anxiety about presenting differently, there are some very common symptoms that many people experience when speaking. Some of the common signs and symptoms of anxiety, according to the Mayo Clinic (2018), include *Feeling Tense, Blushing, Increased Heart rate, Sweating, Breathing Rapidly, Trembling, Gastrointestinal Issues, or Nausea.* These are not the only symptoms, but these are the most commonly experienced by those with speaking anxiety and often are the most intrusive when it comes to speech delivery.

The last thing a speaker wants is physical symptoms to impede their ability to deliver a strong message and to distract the audience from what they are saying. So, what is the solution? Many of these reactions are *uncontrollable*; however, they are *manageable*. What does this mean? A speaker can identify what their physical anxiety response is and consider

Fig 2.1 Feeling nervous can happen during any speech, address the symptoms ahead of time!

Source: https://www.shutterstock.com/image-photo/panoramic-shot-worried-lecturer-suffering-fear-1447332419

ways to soothe or reduce the behaviors. Let's examine each of these reactions and consider possible treatments to reduce these symptoms (Fig. 2.1).

Feeling Tense, Increased Heart rate, Breathing Rapidly: All of these symptoms of anxiety have a treatment in common: deep breathing. According to Dr. James Beckerman with WebMD (2020), deep breathing will not only regulate your breathing rhythms, but it will also help you mentally relax relieving tension. A period of focused breathing will help palpitations subside. For more severe heart rhythms, Dr. Beckerman recommends splashing your face with cold water. This cold shock will stimulate the nerve that regulates your heart rate (2020).

Blushing: Blushing is often a symptom that is uncontrollable and almost untreatable. Some recommendations for preventative measures for speakers who struggle with blushing include not only deep breathing as discussed earlier but also staying hydrated with cool water. Blushing can commonly occur if a speaker gets too hot. Planning the clothing for a presentation can help you from feeling overheated. Wear layers to adapt to the temperature of the room you will speak in, this way if it is warm, you have a cooler layer to present in limiting the chances of becoming red in the face. Some speakers tend to blush when they are anxious without any possible way to prevent or treat it. If this is your tendency, consider wearing clothing that is cooler in color temperature – blacks and dark blues, for example – and avoid wearing something red in tone. The cooler colors will deemphasize your blushing cheeks (and hopefully just create an illusion that you have a tan)!

Sweating: How on earth could someone stop sweating when they aren't even hot? It is impossible. You cannot stop a physiological response, but you can treat it! Dr. Steven J. Heyden (2018), with Aurora Healthcare, has some recommendations to help prepare for anxious sweating. The first recommendation is to carefully choose your clothing. Wear layers that have absorbent or breathable fabrics to reduce moisture collecting and showing on your clothes. Next, consider a stronger or prescription antiperspirant if you feel like you have a medical condition or an extreme sweat response to anxiety. This can eliminate smell and slow the sweating. Go back to earlier recommendations and consider doing some deep breathing to help you be calm and slow your sweat gland reaction to the anxiety (Fig. 2.2).

Gastrointestinal Issues or Nausea: We've all seen that scene in a movie where a character is about to do something great, a performance, play a game, go have a really important meeting and they rush to the restroom sick because they are nervous. Many speakers have the same response, maybe they are not rushing to the restroom, but they are queasy, nauseous, or overall struggling with stomach issues. If this is a common symptom of your speaking anxiety, consider planning ahead when it comes to meals. Heavy or savory meals can sit uncomfortably on your stomach as it is, when you combine this element with nervous nausea it can exaggerate the discomfort experienced. Consider bland or light meals prior to speaking. For example, if the presentation is in the morning, skip the biscuits and gravy with bacon and eggs. Consider something light like toast, fruit, granola, or simple eggs. If the gastrointestinal irritation is more severe, considering having antacids or other medication to take prior to presenting (Fig. 2.3).

Trembling: As previously stated, deep breathing can create calm in your body and mind. However, sometimes this physical response to anxiety is uncontrollable and is very distracting to the audience. If trembling is a response for you when you have speaking anxiety, make sure you are intentional with your hand placement and stance when delivering your speech. Holding on to notes or cards can cause paper to shake and make noise, drawing the audience's eye to your hands and distracting them from your message.

Silas, a student at the University of West Alabama, was very outgoing, likable, and talkative; however, under all his confidence, he was terrified of speaking. During his first presentation in class, his leg was shaking uncontrollably, almost like a person who sits and intentionally bobs their knee up and down as fast as they can to stay focused. One way Silas could have addressed the shaking was to have a firmer stance, planting his feet into the

Fig 2.2 If you are a person who sweats, don't sweat it! Just address it with these tips.

Source: https://www.shutterstock.com/image-photo/
businessman-sweating-his-office-572068330

Fig 2.3 Diagnose your stomach issues when it comes to speaking. Find the solution so you can speak without discomfort.

Source: https://www.shutterstock.com/image-photo/
businessman-holding-his-stomach-pain-326459696

ground. He would have been shaking but not as bad as he was with one foot lightly placed on its toes, rather than firmly flat on the ground.

By the last speech of the semester, Silas stood firmly and calmly without shaking. He was so improved that he was commended for the drastic improvement. When asked what he felt was the reason for the change, he shared that the many opportunities to present helped him not only gain confidence but also familiar with all the elements needed to deliver a good speech. Ultimately, he knew how he felt physically and how he needed to respond to anxiety.

Knowing what to expect from the experience and from yourself when presenting, or *familiarity with presenting*, is the best medicine for anxiety. The best practice for addressing anxiety is rehearsal and regular attempts at speaking. The more opportunities to present, the more familiar you will be with all of the elements, creating a level of confidence each time you speak. While anxiety cannot necessarily be cured it can be managed and addressed to present in a way your reaction does not distract the audience.

Using Physical and Vocal Mechanics to Release Nervous Energy

Speaking Anxiety creates a level of nervous energy that, if left bottled up within us, can evolve into distracting symptoms like trembling, shaking voice, and even rapid breathing. Using mechanics, both vocal and physical, to release this energy is the best way to address possible symptoms and also achieve some best practices of speaking at the same time.

Physical mechanics include using hand gestures, planting feet firmly on the ground to create a good stance, utilizing a podium to anchor hands in place, and having facial expression to engage the audience. These are all small physical actions that can release nervous energy. Vocal mechanics similarly relieve some nervous energy. Boosting volume can keep a voice from shaking and can require lots of physical effort from breathing to speaking in order to shake off some anxiety while you are in the middle of the presentation. A soft voice doesn't require strong breath support and volume, which means nerves stay put. Taking deep breaths, speaking out, and delivering your voice with strong volume can at least present a confident posture without distracting the audience and also the speaker.

Setting Realistic Goals for the Presentation

Being aware of nerves and seeing them manifest into physical symptoms in the middle of a speech can often be the motivating factor for your body to increase or create more speaking anxiety symptoms. This is why setting goals based on *elimination* of symptoms is unrealistic. Many anxious symptoms are incurable and unpredictable. The goal for symptoms must be to *manage* and *anticipate* rather than *eliminate*.

Beyond setting goals related to nerves, it is important to look at small things you can achieve to build your confidence for the next presentation. Small goals like improving volume, building in pauses, avoiding rubble words or slang, speaking slow and steady, and having a strong stance can be achieved and will build significant confidence!

The last thing to prepare for is the worst-case scenario. It is important to ask yourself "what is the worst-case scenario, what's the worst thing that could happen to me during a speech?" Some responses from presenters include fall on the way to the front, throw up, completely go blank during the speech, shake uncontrollably, the list is wide ranging, and each one has an action plan you can develop. Shaking? Don't hold your notes, stand firm! Throw up? First, that is a rare occurrence, and second, remember to plan ahead: eat light, take antacids! Fall on the way to the stage? Well, have a self-depricating joke ready. Say something about how you clearly cannot wait to share your speech! Go blank in the middle of the speech? That's what notes are for!

Regardless of your level of anxiety about speaking, we all have some nerves at times; otherwise we are lying to ourselves. Self-evaluation is the key to addressing the matter of nerves. Ask yourself: What is my symptom? How can I address it? What is my worst-case scenario? What would my response be before and after nerves begin to build? What goals can I set for my presentation that are realistic? Mental and physical preparation is the key to building confidence and addressing nerves before they spiral out of control. Don't avoid the work, ask the hard questions of yourself, and have an action plan so you can deliver an effective message without distracting your audience.

References

"Anxiety Disorders." Mayo Clinic. Mayo Foundation for Medical Education and Research, May 4, 2018. https://www.mayoclinic.org/diseases-conditions/anxiety/symptoms-causes/syc-20350961.

Beckerman, James. "What to Do If Your Heart Races, Slows Down, or Skips a Beat." WebMD. WebMD, August 24, 2020. https://www.webmd.com/heart-disease/atrial-fibrillation/what-to-do-heart-races.

Seinfeld, Jerry. *Jerry Seinfeld: I'm Telling You for the Last Time.* United States: HBO, 1998.

"Why Do People Sweat When Nervous? 6 Ways to Stop It." Aurora Health Care. Accessed January 12, 2021. https://www.aurorahealthcare.org/patients-visitors/blog/why-do-people-sweat-when-nervous-6-ways-to-stop-it.

TAKE ACTION

Answer the following questions to start mentally preparing for the next presentation you have!

1. What are your most common symptoms to anxiety or nerves, especially when presenting?

   _____

   _____

2. What are some solutions you can implement to manage the symptoms?

   _____

   _____

3. What is the worst-case scenario you have playing in your head as you consider your upcoming presentation?

   _____

   _____

4. What could you do to respond before or after to this worst-case scenario?

   _____

   _____

5. Write down some small goals you would like to achieve. These can be about how you present or about nerves but must be achievable to build your confidence!

   _____

   _____

3 Physical Mechanics

> "There is no such thing as presentation talent, it is called presentation skills"
>
> *—David JP Phillips*

If a speaker doesn't consider the physical elements of public speaking, they will often fail at achieving delivery style and vocal mechanics required to be a dynamic speaker. Physical mechanics are the foundation from which a presenter builds the best practices of speaking. Each element of a speaker's physical mechanics promotes strength in other areas of presenting. The four different physical mechanics that impact a presentation are *Stance, Eye Contact, Facial Expression,* and *Gestures.* Each one of these is important to implement into a presentation in order to hold a confident posture while speaking.

Stance

Stance is the positioning of the body and feet while doing an activity according to Merriam-Webster Dictionary (2020). A presenter must achieve a strong stance while speaking. How you stand is important, not only to show that you are confident but also to help you breathe deep and strong, which in turn allows you to project your voice. Breath support begins in the diaphragm, found in your abdomen (Fig. 3.1). If a speaker

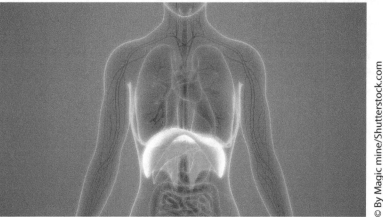

© By Magic mine/Shutterstock.com

Fig 3.1 The location of the diaphragm is right at the natural waist. As you can see any leaning or bending will collapse or limit the capacity for strong breath control.

Source: https://www.shutterstock.com/image-illustration/human-body-organs-diaphragm-anatomy-3d-1027391245

15

is hunched over or leans on a podium, the diaphragm is bent or closed off, making it difficult to get a strong breath that ultimately limits the volume a speaker can achieve. Having strong deep breath also helps calm nerves and limit shakiness of the voice.

What is the proper way to stand? Many inexperienced speakers tend to wander on a stage or sway back and forth. Having a poor stance that includes this kind of movement can be very distracting to the audience. A strong stance is not just about how you place your feet on the floor, it runs from the head to the toes. Starting at the foundation of your stance, the lower body, a speaker should stand with feet firmly planted, no more or less than hip width apart and avoid locking the knees back. The upper body should be tall and open, with shoulders rolled back, and straight. You may have been reminded a time or two to "put your shoulders back" by a very persistent friend or mother. Hunched shoulders can lead to leaning forward, hurting breath support, and can signal insecurity to the audience. So, if all else fails, "put your shoulders back!" Once your shoulders are square, the last piece is to set your head in a natural space. Do not look up or down, have your chin at a natural level. How does one know the natural level? Imagine a string running up your spine through the crown of your head to angle your eye and chin level to the proper placement. This will keep your gaze straight ahead and coordinated with your body and encourage strong eye contact (Fig. 3.2).

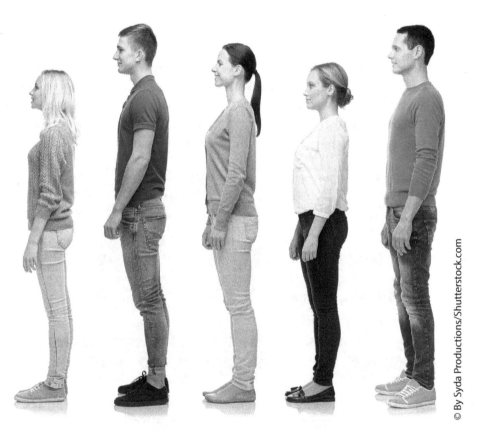

© By Syda Productions/Shutterstock.com

Fig 3.2 Notice each person with a strong natural stance, no matter your size or body type you can achieve a strong stance from head to toe.

Source: https://www.shutterstock.com/image-photo/group-people-side-367351289

Eye Contact

Audiences need to trust a speaker. The easiest way to gain the audience's trust and convey confidence is to have strong eye contact. Many people struggle with being comfortable looking at a stranger in the audience eye to eye for many seconds. Sometimes it can distract a speaker from what they are saying. An often-ill-advised solution that people offer is to suggest the speaker look at the back wall of the room. The problem with staring at the wall is that people start to look over their shoulder thinking something is happening behind them. Dropping the gaze to be more eye level with an audience member appears more natural. Work to rest your gaze on an audience member for 2–3 seconds at a time. If there is a familiar face, a friend, or a family member in the audience, start by looking their way first to get some confidence as those people will always be pleasant to look at and put you at ease. Being at ease will allow you to have a pleasant expression as you look at each person.

Facial Expression

Speakers can connect emotionally with the audience through strong proper facial expression. A raised eyebrow, bright smile, strong frown, and so much more can communicate between the spoken phrases and can enhance the spoken word with a face that shares a specific emotion. Comedians are excellent communicators with simple facial expressions between jokes and while people are laughing. It communicates what they are thinking and connects them to the audience. The importance is to be mindful of how you are using your face if at all and understand it can still communicate emotion even if it is not the speaker's intention. Many times, people think they should always smile, but smiling may not be appropriate. Imagine a presenter standing on stage with a bright happy smile and their opening line is, "How would you feel if I told you that you have 3 months to live?" As someone in the audience looks on and ties the words together with the bright happy smile, they may think poorly of the speaker, who is communicating with insensitive facial expression to all watching in that moment! Maybe a speaker is nervous, they have a tense-focused face, but the topic is happy. They stand, brow furrowed with a strong frown, and begin, "Going to college can be the most cherished 4 years of your life." This is not very believable with the face being so negative in its expression. You can see how using facial expression is important to communicate and enhance a presentation properly, and if used incorrectly it can hurt the overall message. Using a smile or some facial expression is one of the easiest and quickest ways to improve a presentation.

Gestures

There is a moment in the 2006 film *Talladega Nights: The Ballad of Ricky Bobby* in which the lead character Ricky being interviewed by the media starts to slowly raise his hands up to his face. He tells the reporter, "I don't know what to do with my hands." The reporter responds, "It'd be good just to hold them to your side." But Ricky just continues to raise his hands and the reporter reaches out to slowly push the hands back down. Some presenters fully identify with Ricky Bobby; they just do not know where to put their hands.

© By Roman Samborskyi/Shutterstock.com

Fig 3.3 Don't know what to do with your hands? It'd be good just to hold your hands to your sides.

Source: https://www.shutterstock.com/image-photo/not-my-problem-photo-beautiful-dark-1577796727

The best placement for your hands is simple; however, it seems like it is often *too simple* for some presenters. Not doing something with the hands seems too basic and subtly challenges presenters as they prepare their speech (Fig. 3.3).

It *would* be best just to hold your hands to your sides; however, if you are a fidgety person or really need to have something for your hands to do, there are some simple solutions. First, if you have a podium or a table, resting your hands on each side or holding the edges is a good way to fill your hands with something that is not distracting to the audience. Conversely, holding a prop or any paper notes in your hands will distract the audience as your hands may shake causing noise, or you may wave the paper around as you move your hands, almost like waving a surrender flag. Maybe you have important points to emphasize. Intentional and purposeful gestures are an excellent way to grab the audience's attention to follow what you are presenting.

What is the best way to put gestures in a presentation? In other words, what do you do with your hands? Make sure your hand placement coordinates with what you are saying. For example, if you are saying directional words like up, down, left, or right, point or indicate with your hands in the same direction. If you say "you" when talking to the audience or "me" talking about yourself, use your hands to signal who you are talking about. The goal is to compliment the phrases you say, not overpower what you say. Using big arm movements should be limited to big phrasing. There's nothing more awkward than seeing a presenter wave hands around like they are surrendering. Second, make sure you work to keep your hands placed in an area we will call *home base*. Imagine the section of space from your shoulders down to your waist as a place to anchor most of your gestures. In the 2006 film *Hitch*, the main character Alfred Hitchens is teaching his client, Albert, to dance. After watching a very poor display of dancing from Albert, where he flails his arms around embarrassingly, Hitch limits his dancing from side to side with hands very close to his hips. As Hitch says to Albert, "You live here," the same goes for your home base, your gestures live there, your gestures must live between your shoulders and waist throughout the presentation.

The best way to incorporate these gestures is to plan for them early and use them from the beginning of your efforts in rehearsing. If they are part of the rehearsal, they will translate more naturally on stage. If there is still some apprehension about using big gestures, plan for natural placement on a podium or "it'd be good just to hold them to your side."

The physical mechanics of a presentation require practice. While some speakers are gifted with some natural talent, most speakers must develop these skills through intentional rehearsal and evaluation each time they present. If a speaker is able to develop strong physical mechanics, they will have a strong foundation allowing them to have impactful and purposeful presentations.

References

Hitch. Film. New York, NY: Columbia, 2005.

McKay, Adam, and Will Ferrell. *Talladega Nights: the Ballad of Ricky Bobby*. Film. United States: Sony Pictures Entertainment, 2006.

"Stance." Merriam-Webster. Accessed January 12, 2021. https://www.merriam-webster.com/dictionary/stance?src=search-dict-box.

TAKE ACTION

Stand in front of a mirror, and practice your stance. Feet hip width apart, roll your shoulders back to open your chest, take a deep breath, and straighten your neck.

1. How does it feel?

    _____

2. If it feels weird or uncomfortable, what part is the hardest to maintain?

    _____

Check out your facial expression, practice smiling and frowning, and check out how your face looks.

1. Does it look forced or natural?

    _____

2. Make adjustments, what can you improve or change to be more natural with your face?

    _____

In the short timeframe, make sure that you practice your stance, facial expression, gestures, and eye contact. Video yourself to evaluate these mechanics and make adjustments each time you practice!

4 | Vocal Mechanics

Physical mechanics are only half the battle of engaging your audience. How you present the words out loud is the other half. Improper or lack of use of vocal mechanics can negate all the good physical mechanics have achieved in your presentation. Energy flows from the mouth of the presenter. Likewise, energy is stopped in its tracks with the voice. Without strong vocal mechanics, a speaker will limit the impact their words have on the audience. The elements essential to build strong vocal mechanics are *Tone, Pitch, Intonation, Volume, Rate, and Pauses.*

Tone, Pitch, and Intonation

Tone and pitch go hand in hand, changes in vocal pitch can create a specific tone. The various definitions in Merriam Webster's Dictionary (2020) for the word *tone* include *the pitch of a word often used to express differences of meaning; a sound of definite pitch or vibration; manner of expression when speaking; accent or inflection expressive of a mood or emotion.* These definitions clearly show that tone is necessary to convey feelings and meaning beyond bringing the words on the page to life. Maya Angelou says this perfectly, "Words mean more than what is set down on paper. It takes the human voice to infuse them with shades of deeper meaning" (1979) Presentation notes are shorter than an essay on the same topic because more detailed clarification and explanation must occur in text. However, when someone speaks, inflection, emphasis, and the rise and fall of pitch all indicate the thoughts and meaning behind the words without further need for explanation. Consider this sentence:

<u>Ella</u> didn't <u>ride</u> <u>her</u> <u>bike</u> to <u>school</u>.

If you read this sentence emphasizing with a strong tone only one of the underlined words while saying the rest very neutral, the sentence has five different meanings. For example, if you emphasize the word *bike* it means that Ella rode something other than a bike to school. But if you emphasize the word *her* it means Ella rode someone else's bike. Tone and a high or low pitch can completely alter a sentence and offer a backstory that doesn't require more details. A change in tone and pitch is worth a thousand words.

Intonation is the use of tone and pitch while speaking. In order to understand intonation, imagine a sound file, much like the one pictured in Fig. 4.1. Have you ever used Soundcloud or a Voice Memo and seen the waves move up and down as you play the file? This is a visual picture of intonation, the pattern of the rise, and fall of your pitch and tone as you speak.

Conversely, lacking intonation looks much like a flat-lined sound file. If you were asked what flat line on any file or monitor indicates, you would probably respond with "dead" or "dead air." We must avoid having our voices be a flat line much like the one you see in Fig 4.2. Energy flows from the mouth, so strong intonation must be paired with our

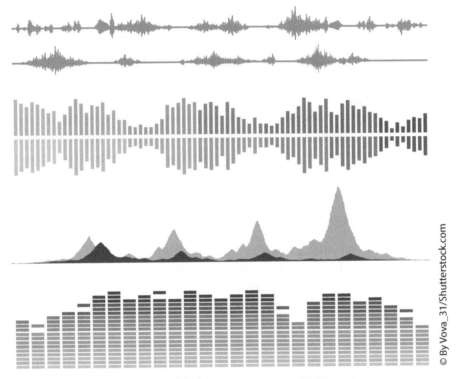

© By Vova_31/Shutterstock.com

Fig 4.1 Notice these various sound wave files. As you can see each file has different peaks and valleys which show how the sound rises and falls naturally.

Source: https://www.shutterstock.com/image-vector/sound-waves-set-music-background-eps-749619469

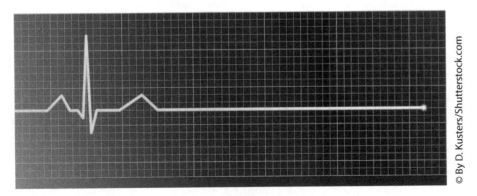

© By D. Kusters/Shutterstock.com

Fig 4.2 Don't let your voice flat line leaving the audience hopeless. Use Pitch, Tone, and Intonation to create peaks and valleys in your voice.

Source: https://www.shutterstock.com/image-illustration/heart-pulse-monitor-flatline-raster-version-87801649

content in order to move and impact people with those words we have crafted. In the 1986 film *Ferris Bueller's Day Off*, Ferris skips school and as his teacher is calling roll, you can experience what a speaker who lacks strong intonation sounds like! The teacher, in a low, monotone sound calls each student. When he gets to Ferris, he says "Bueller... Bueller... Bueller..." all the same tone, no rise to indicate the question mark, all causing the class to fall asleep before it starts. Avoid being this kind of speaker. Be lively with your tone, pitch, and intonation to emphasize the shades of deeper meaning behind your words.

There are some negative, culturally influenced, forms of intonation that often are picked up and can negatively reflect on the speaker. Two we will discuss are *Vocal Fry* and *Uptalk*.

Vocal Fry, often referred to as "Kardashian voice," is a low-vibration sounding like creaking in the voice often at the end of a phrase. The speaker, if using vocal fry, will sound disengaged, underwhelmed, and bored. According to her 2013 CBS Sunday Morning report *On Vocal Fry*, Faith Salle tells us that research has shown that millennials who use vocal fry are seen as "urban oriented and upwardly mobile." While your peer group may see you as progressive with your intonation, that does not always mean you will be celebrated when using this form of speaking. Being a presenter often leads us to diverse audiences who may not have the same perspective. One of the most common speeches people will have to make is a job interview and often the interviewer can be from a different background, culture, and generation, which could lead them to negatively receive a potential employee who uses vocal fry.

Uptalk is another form of negative intonation from the 1980s and 1990s but still is heard among speakers. Often nicknamed "Valley Girl," uptalk is an intonation that rises up at the end of each statement. Going up on your tone at the end of the statement often translates to the listener like the statement is a question. People using uptalk sound like they are unsure of what they are saying to the audience. For example, if I use uptalk when I say, "College is the best 4 years of your life." It sounds like, "College is the best 4 years of your life?" This intonation prompts the audience to subconsciously ask back, "Is it really?," which ultimately impacts the presenter's credibility.

Often, negative intonation is a product of influence. Meaning, we will sound like the individuals we surround ourselves with. Because we tend to lean our intonation toward that of our peers, listening for intonation among the group will help you identify what may be a commonly used intonation or verbiage in their own way of speaking. If the actual issue is still hard to diagnose, recording a speech and listening back may help you notice areas for improvement with your tone, pitch, and intonation.

Lastly, work to round out your tone, pitch, and intonation into the lower levels of your voice. Now, that doesn't mean speak with your best Morgan Freeman impression; it means to speak at the deepest level of your voice that is comfortable. The reason behind this is that lower voices indicate leadership ability and give the speaker credibility. For women, this is more of a struggle as they can naturally have a higher register to their voice. So, to avoid overdoing this deep tone, consider this scenario: When a parent or a teacher has to discipline someone, they often get a serious deep tone to their voice. The recommendation, especially to women, is to use your "mom voice" or "teacher voice" to get into the mindset of using a lower pitch and tone while presenting.

Using the tools of tone, pitch, and intonation will allow for strong expression of meaning and ideas in your presentation. Lacking in this element of vocal mechanics leaves an impact on how the content's meaning is communicated and limits the ability of the speaker to connect with the audience.

Volume

In the 1993 *Puffy Shirt* episode of the television show *Seinfeld*, there is a character that has been dubbed a "low talker." The lead characters, Jerry and Elaine, go on a double date with their friend Kramer and his date Leslie. Every time Leslie responds to a question, she mumbles almost incoherently. Jerry and Elaine nod along like they may understand, but by the end of the conversation she gets Jerry to unknowingly agree to wear a hideous puffy shirt she designed for his next comedy show. Often, presenters do this very thing to their audience; they think the audience leaning in to hear them actually means the people are engaged; however, they will ultimately lose the audience if they cannot hear. Regardless of the setting, it is important for presenters to project their voice to create energy and engage the audience.

How loud do I need to be? The recommendation is that if you feel like you are speaking loud enough, that means you need to go up one more level in volume. Using the room to gauge volume is also helpful. The bigger the room you are presenting in, the louder you should speak. Some people have a naturally quiet voice; however, it still is possible for all speakers to achieve strong volume, or projection, by engaging their diaphragm. The diaphragm is the section in the lower abdomen that can be considered much like a trampoline for your breathing, allowing you to achieve strong volume. Think about cheerleaders and how they shout cheers over and over weekly and usually never lose their voice, or famous singers who hit high notes in a ballad and still can perform nightly. They engage their abdominal muscles and use the diaphragm to force air over their vocal chords to boost the volume. This can be achieved by deep breathing into the abdomen rather than shallow breathing. The best way to see if you are achieving deep breath is to observe if your chest is rising or your abdomen is rising when taking a breath in. If only the chest is rising, breath will be shallow, limiting volume and running out of air sooner than if the abdomen is used. The best way to test deeper breathing is to place hands on the lower stomach and breathe deep to where the hand lifts outward. If your stomach rises, you are breathing deep and will sustain your air longer and be able to achieve strong volume.

To project your voice, imagine your words coming out of your mouth like a beam of light to project a movie on the back wall of the room. Imagine shooting your words to the wall with such force that they bounce back to you. This is projection; much like a real projector, the goal is to fill up a wall with the full picture in a clear way. Projection not only gives strong volume but also creates energy in the room that captures the audience's interest and attention. Have you ever watched a presentation where the first words out of the presenter's mouth were loud and booming and energetic? Anytime a presenter starts this way the whole room will sit up a little straighter, looking up from notes to check out what this speech is about, and that attention stays as the speaker maintains the volume and energy.

Rate

Rate is how fast one speaks. The rate of speaking should be slower than a presenter usually talks in a normal setting. Some presenters have a very high rate of speaking naturally, which, when paired with nerves, can cause them to kick into overdrive and speed up beyond anything natural. How do you avoid talking fast? If you know you have a naturally fast rate when you present, make reminders on your notes, and practice speaking at half speed. Build in intentional pauses. Intentionally closing lips all the way and making sure each mark of punctuation is a place for a pause, and a breath is the best way to slow down rate.

Pauses

So many presenters struggle to be comfortable with silence. When someone stands in front of people, it is almost as is time stands still and a 3-second pause can seem like an eternity. However, a short pause can allow the audience to stay in step with the spoken word, absorb what they just heard, and go unnoticed. A presenter will choose one of two options if they do not build in space for pauses: really fast rate or rubble words.

Rubble Words are those words that fill in all the holes between phrases, little scraps of verbiage that are not part of the completed structure of content in a speech. Imagine a house being built, a foundation, walls, all the materials used often have little pieces tossed in the rubble pile and when the house is fully built these are pieces placed to the side ready for the dumpster.

Another way to think of rubble words is like the spinning dots or a buffering signal on a computer. The user is clicking so fast that the computer has not caught up to the command. The same thing happens when we speak too fast and do not implement proper pauses and a slow rate; the rubble word is what our mouths say while we buffer waiting for the brain to send our next phrase to our mouths. We must speak at a slow and steady rate with intentional pauses so we can synchronize our minds with our words.

Do you know your Rubble word? In the 2014 article, *10 Hardest Habits to Break,* (Freeman) 3 of the 10 hardest habits are all verbal. Negative verbal habits are very difficult to break and master as they have become a signature of our communication. Even Biblical scripture cites how difficult it is to master our words:

> *"When we put bits into the mouths of horses to make them obey us, we can turn the whole animal. Or take ships as an example. Although they are so large and are driven by strong winds, they are steered by a very small rudder wherever the pilot wants to go. Likewise, the tongue is a small part of the body, but it makes great boasts. Consider what a great forest is set on fire by a small spark." James 3:3-5*

James, the writer of this verse compares the tongue to small items that can completely correct the course of an animal or a ship or even set a whole forest on fire. Likewise with common slang or rubble words, they can completely change the course of the speech when used; this is why it is so important to work to identify what words you use so you can start the work early.

The first step to breaking this habit is to ask someone close to you to tell you what this word could be. Common rubble words include *like, you know, umm, so, ok, you know what I'm saying* and are used frequently between phrases and even multiple times in a sentence. Avoiding silence and pauses using rubble words can make a presenter look unprepared, unpolished, unprofessional, and hurt their credibility. For example, Caroline Kennedy while running for senate in 2008 was virtually laughed off the campaign trail for using "you know" 51 times in a New York 1 cable news interview, and again using "you know"

142 times in an interview with the *New York Times* (Thompson, 2008, para 4,5). While Caroline Kennedy may have spoken like some of the New Yorkers she would represent, they still did not want their political representative to sound like them, they wanted her to sound better and more professional to fit the position she was seeking to fill. People want leaders, representatives, and presenters to be polished and professional. Rubble words will lend themselves to undermine credibility and could impact jobs if used in a professional setting.

Do not give short shrift to the vocal mechanics of a presentation. Attack the speech in a way that creates "shades of deeper meaning" to the words you are saying. Build energy and enthusiasm for your presentation by working to develop strong vocal mechanics. Let the energy flow from your voice to ensure you impact the audience, leaving them wanting to hear your next presentation.

References

Freeman, Shanna. "10 Hardest Habits to Break." HowStuffWorks. July 13, 2014. https://health.howstuffworks.com/mental-health/human-nature/behavior/10-hardest-habits-break.htm.

Angelou, Maya. 1979. *I know why the caged bird sings.* New York: Random House.

Hughes, John, Tom Jacobson, Matthew Broderick, Alan Ruck, Mia Sara, Jeffrey Jones, Jennifer Grey, et al. 1987. *Ferris Bueller's day off.* Hollywood, CA: Paramount Pictures Corp.

James 3:3-5; New International Version, Retrieved from Biblegateway.com https://www.cbsnews.com/amp/video/faith-salie-on-speaking-with-vocal-fry/

TAKE ACTION

1. Stand tall and breathe deep with your hands on your abdomen. Force air out quickly while shouting "HA!" If you can't strongly shout that, try again. Work to gain strong volume and projection. Practice this exercise a few times until you feel confident in your volume.

2. What is your Rubble Word? _____

3. Who can you ask to keep you accountable when you say this word? Write their name here and ask them to help you! _____

4. List some scenarios where you can practice eliminating your rubble word(s) (e.g., job fair, conversations with professor or boss, on the phone). Commit to practicing eliminating this bad habit. _____

_____

_____

5 | Presentation Methods

Using the right method for a presentation is the key to making sure that the overall goals of the presentation and proper delivery are achieved. Just as when a recipe calls for the chef to fry versus sauté chicken, the outcome of the overall quality, taste, and likability of the dish can be compromised if the wrong method was used to cook the protein. Likewise, with a presentation, using the wrong method could compromise the impact of the presentation on the audience and the presenter themselves. The method chosen can greatly increase the time needed for preparation and curation of content, and the delivery of the presentation can be inappropriate and poorly received. This limits credibility and likability with the audience.

When approaching a presentation, the setting, the audience, and the content itself will help a presenter choose a method. There are four core methods of presenting to choose from: *Manuscript, Memorized, Impromptu, and Extemporaneous.* All four methods are needed for specific situations and audiences. Choose the wrong method and the process of building and delivering a speech can directly affect the overall presentation.

Manuscript Method

When you hear the word manuscript, what comes to mind? Old, historical looking handwritten documents maybe? This may be one of the oldest, tried, and true methods for crafting and delivering a speech (Fig. 5.1). The Manuscript Method is best used in

Fig 5.1 The manuscript method is the most time intensive method to utilize when creating a presentation.

scenarios where a specific message must be shared word for word. That is, where the presenter must not go off script for reasons of time, legality, or professionalism. For example, if a professional must terminate an employee, they might be given a script to follow for legal reasons. Should they add to that script, it could open up their company to liability or legal action from the employee being let go. If a company must deliver a message in the face of a disaster or an emergency, their spokesperson must follow the script to avoid any repercussions of saying something incorrect or inaccurate (legal or otherwise).

Using the Manuscript method is not recommended for most speakers as it takes so much time to prepare and often limits the speaker in their ability to deliver a dynamic presentation. This method is quite time intensive because it requires that every word spoken is written down prior to being rehearsed. This step of scripting the content delays the efforts to begin rehearsal, which means the presenter must begin early in order to thoroughly prepare for the presentation. A Manuscript presentation also can impact an inexperienced presenter in terms of delivery. Most speakers cannot write content in a way that is pleasing to the listener. Often the content is written for reading not hearing. Delivery will sound robotic and stiff if written in this manner.

The Manuscript method is best used for shorter presentations like an introduction, a brief statement, or acceptance speech. If a presentation calls for the need of a specific message that must be scripted, presenters should work to rehearse early and often in order to have a conversational style and have confidence in their message.

Memorized

Memorized, while also a scripted method of presenting, is even more difficult and time consuming than a Manuscript presentation because it takes all the preparation of the Manuscript method and then requires the presenter memorize the content and recite it word for word without notes or a script with them on the day of the presentation. This is the most time-intensive method of preparation and is not recommended for most speeches. The risk presenters take using a Memorized method of presenting is they could lose their words or go blank in front of the audience. The lack of notes or a script combined with nerves can often cause presenters to forget what they want to say and without the notes, there is nothing to help them get back on track when they go blank. If the situation calls for a presenter to deliver a speech without notes, the Memorized method should be used. Typically, speeches such as an introduction, toasts, or an acceptance speech or thank you are often delivered with a Memorized method. Any presentation longer than a minute or two should not use the Memorized method.

Impromptu

If you were asked what impromptu means, you may say on the spot, on the fly, or off the top of your head. While this is accurate, it does not mean you cannot prepare for impromptu situations when it comes to speaking. What are the situations that may call for impromptu speaking? Interviews, question and answer sessions, conference room meetings, and any situation where you may be expected to provide answers or input are impromptu-speaking opportunities.

How could anyone prepare for an impromptu-speaking opportunity? First is by knowing yourself. Understanding what you think about things, having a clear idea in your mind what your opinions are, and why you have them will shape how you speak in impromptu situations. Second, anticipate impromptu-speaking opportunities. There are opportunities that happen because of a profession or activity or even a current event. For example, professional athlete NFL quarterback Tom Brady will know that the media will ask questions in a press conference, on the sidelines after the game, or even out in public. Each scenario would still require impromptu speaking. In a press conference, he may need to consider the upcoming game, the opponent and their strengths, have a phrase or statement about teammates, coaches, and the planning and preparation being done that week, all of these things he can plan for in advance, many times he may have the same statement for certain questions no matter what the situation is that week. Curating potential responses based on his profession and activities while considering current events (such as opponents, injuries, and big plays or failures that week) will provide content Brady needs when faced with an impromptu situation for speaking.

While most individuals do not find themselves in the situation of weekly interviews with the press like Tom Brady, everyone will face job interviews, which are of great importance when pursing a new job. While oftentimes an interview will follow a normal routine with commonly asked questions, there are some rare employers that like to ask unique questions that an interviewee may have never expected. Knowing the common questions and even researching some unique questions will prepare you to provide well-spoken and thoughtful answers rather than letting a good bit of awkward silence pass while you try to form an answer on the spot.

How do we prepare? **Here's a question to practice with: "A recent poll shows that a fifth of Americans can't locate the US on a world map. Why do you think this is?"**

First, what would you consider as possible topics to help answer this question, specifically ones you are knowledgeable about? Maybe education. What about Technology? The fading practice of using paper maps, or Geography in schools. Any of these and maybe more that come to *your mind* might be what you consider as you answer this question, basing your response on what you know in these topic areas.

This very question was delivered during the televised 2007 Miss Teen USA pageant. It is very possible to prepare for questions in this situation. Every pageant will have an interview portion off camera and by the time contestants are interviewed on television, they have already successfully completed at least one round of questions that same week as well as other rounds of similar interviews during the pageants they have competed in to qualify for the national-level pageant. When preparing for the interview portion of any pageant, impromptu methods must be implemented. Evaluating types of questions to form answers is key to being successful. Current events are always topics that will be discussed along with personal passions and purposes in a pageant interview. During this moment in the 2007 contest, Miss South Carolina Teen USA, Caitlin Upton, found herself facing thousands of people in the audience not to mention the millions watching at home. Allowing nerves to take over, she spends her 30 seconds rambling about nothing that truly addresses the question. Why? Because she didn't have a rehearsed response about a topic ready. But how would she know this specific topic? She might not; however, she would know her stance on general issues like education or technology and bridge the question into an answer that is based on that topic not necessarily the exact question.

Let's go back and answer the Miss Teen USA question for her: Maybe you are the most familiar with technology, so your response could be something like this: *"One of the reasons could be that **many of us utilize and depend on technology** more than ever. If someone needs directions, they no longer have to find their location on a map, they simply type in where they want to go, and a GPS system will create a route for them. Not seeing a full map, and more specifically, only caring about what pops up on the screen limits our population's ability to know or even care about maps or even the world outside their device."* While this answer does mention maps, it is not about geography or maps at all; it is about the negative impact of technology on society bridged to apply it to a question about maps (Fig. 5.2).

The impromptu method isn't about knowing the correct answer when asked questions or called upon to speak. It is about knowing your personal perspective and point of view and answering in a way that reflects those things to the audience. Every listener will assess the presentation based on their own personal opinions, however, the speech you give must come from your knowledge and interests; otherwise it will miss the mark.

Fig 5.2 No matter the situation, impromptu speaking is something we can prepare for.

Source: https://www.shutterstock.com/image-photo/miss-universe-denmark-2016-on-stage-472990249

© By Face of Denmark/Shutterstock.com

Extemporaneous

The most commonly used method of speaking is Extemporaneous speaking. This method combines a set of well-researched notes (not a script) with conversational tone to achieve a natural delivery style. A key characteristic of the Extemporaneous method is that it achieves efficiency in areas of preparation and practice. Content is not scripted; rather it uses an outline with abbreviated cues that remind a presenter what they want to say. With more time to rehearse the content, a more conversational style will be achieved because it is well practiced and the presenter is not obligated to follow every word on the page (Fig. 5.3).

Utilizing the correct method for the situation and audience will be essential when working to achieve dynamic delivery. Extemporaneous method is very beneficial to the presenter as it supports dynamic delivery in many different ways: by supporting

Fig 5.3 Extemporaneous method uses notes and promotes dynamic delivery.

Source: https://www.shutterstock.com/image-photo/young-caucasian-business-woman-looking-speaker-1866921802

conversational style, allowing for flexibility with content, and creating more time for rehearsal. With less rigorous preparation of content, extemporaneous speakers are able to begin practice of the speech much sooner than those who choose to fully script their content with the manuscript method. By only utilizing a set of notes, the presenter will only have to build out visual cues to remind themselves of the next point on the outline and they will deliver content without staring down at a page. Spending less time on writing out content will allow rehearsal to get started sooner. Using notes encourages a more conversational style as it does not provide the crutch of having every word written down. Many presenters feel like they must say every word on a page when it is there, taking that hindrance away will promote a conversational tone and style. While the phrasing used may be different from rehearsal to rehearsal, it will still sound more natural and approachable than a scripted presentation.

Often the situation calls for different or additional examples, stories, or ideas to be shared in the presentation. The extemporaneous method is more flexible than the others in this scenario. With simply an outline, there is no need to worry about how to fit in new information or content; one would just include the new items as the topic comes up in the structure of the presentation.

Regardless of the situation and the audience, there are many choices for a presentation method. The key is choosing the correct method to achieve the best delivery style and connect with the audience.

TAKE ACTION

Can you deliver a 60-second impromptu response to a question? Try it out! Select a topic below and spend about a minute to prepare and then deliver a speech under 60 seconds using your personal knowledge and opinion to create your speech! Remember when you have a prompt that allows for a single response (like a best vacation or dessert), say more than just a single response, give your personal perspective as support for your choice.

TOPICS:

- What would you do if you won the lottery?
- What subject do you think should be taught in high school that they don't teach?
- What is the best dessert?
- Where would you recommend a couple go on a honeymoon vacation?
- What would you say is the best way to eat an Oreo cookie?
- Recommend a safe vehicle for a family to purchase.
- Which is better? Country or city living?
- At what age should a person be able to begin using a smartphone/social media?
- Should the legal drinking age be changed? Why?
- Who is the best professional athlete of all time?
- If you could play any sport professionally, what would you play? Why?
- What would you say is the best movie of all time?
- What is the best ride at Disney World?
- Who do you most admire and why?

6 | Purpose of Presentations

Having purpose in a presentation is one of the core facets needed to create a fully realized topic. A presenter must identify the *general purpose, the specific purpose,* and the *behavioral purpose* of their presentation to fully achieve a clear and focused topic.

General Purpose

The first step is to consider the general purpose of the presentation. There are three major general purposes the presenter can use: *Informative, Persuasive, and Entertainment.* Understanding what your general purpose is often will be detailed in an assignment or the invitation to present.

Informative

The first general purpose for a presentation is to inform. Informative presentations are aimed at explaining, demonstrating, showing, and ultimately teaching details about a specific topic. By the end of the presentation, the audience should clearly understand the topic. This purpose should ultimately enlighten listeners about a specific topic.

Informative presentations can naturally diffuse tension regarding controversial topics by utilizing supporting material to provide evidence behind their explanation of a specific topic. However, informative presentations can run the risk of being boring because of so much detail. It is important that the presenter builds in examples, metaphors, or even analogies to take high-level information to a more general level of knowledge for the audience. While informative presentations are specifically about factual details of an event or concept, the presenter may provide evidence to support their own personal perspective on the topic.

Persuasive

Persuasive presentations are aimed at not only enlightening listeners on a topic but focused on changing beliefs, actions, or attitudes of those listeners. Being clear about the specific side of an issue or topic is key for the presenter in order to create clarity about the presentation's purpose. To achieve this clarity, knowing the exact way you want a listener's perspective to be swayed is important. To diffuse controversy, a persuasive speech should include facts and statistics and other supporting material to provide a foundation for the presenter's position on the topic. Showing strong research to support your position will build your credibility with the audience and for your position.

Entertainment

The Entertainment purpose sets goals to entertain the listener and make a topic more enjoyable. Inspirational presentations as well as motivational presentations can fall under the purpose of entertainment. Any type of presentation aimed at capturing the audience's attention and encouraging them or providing enjoyment would be considered an entertainment purpose. This often is more of a secondary purpose paired with either informing or persuading. Often evening presentations will need entertainment as part of their general purpose to capture the audience's attention (Fig 6.1).

Specific Purpose

Once you identify the general purpose, you will need to consider the specific purpose of the speech, that is, what *you* hope to accomplish with your overall presentation. When selecting a topic, there is always some level of opinion or bias from a presenter's perspective and the content will be approached from that perspective and must be clarified in the specific purpose statement. The concrete goal a presenter wishes to achieve is clarified with specific verbiage based on the general purpose. For example, an informative presentation's goals are to teach an audience so utilizing words such as *explain, show, demonstrate, describe,* and of course *inform* will highlight the specific purpose. Persuasive presentations may use words such as *motivate, persuade, or convince* in the specific purpose.

Fig 6.1 Entertainment requires enthusiasm and showmanship.

Source: https://www.shutterstock.com/image-photo/famous-entertainer-gets-on-stage-greets-1746589316

Behavioral Purpose

The behavioral purpose is aimed at identifying the specific behaviors you want your audience to have in response to your presentation. If you want them to quit doing something like smoking, then you would indicate that in your overall thesis statement. If you want them to support a cause or understand something more clearly you will identify this specifically in your overall purpose and state it in your thesis. When a general purpose is to inform, behavioral purposes may include the audience being able to do a new task or fully explain a new concept, whereas if the general purpose is to persuade, the audience may choose to take action or have a new attitude or a shift in beliefs about the overall topic (Fig. 6.2).

Fig 6.2 The audience is one of the most important pieces to the puzzle of creating your purpose.

Source: https://www.shutterstock.com/image-photo/adult-people-conference-listen-woman-speaker-1575559552

Questions to Ask

It's always important to ask yourself some very critical questions of your goals when trying to identify and achieve a purpose. Here are some questions you can ask:

- What does the assignment or presentation invitation say I am supposed to use for my general purpose?

- What are my overall goals for this presentation?

Once you've answered these questions and some of the answers may include a full list of items that you want to achieve, then critically evaluate the information you've put down on paper and ask further questions about your specific purpose like these:

- What do I want my audience to do in response to my presentation? Do I want them to learn something or do I want them to change an attitude belief or action?

- What topic interests me? What am I passionate about? What current events am I following?

- What is my current position on this particular topic?

Once you've answered these questions, you may have a more accurate idea of what kind of topic you'd like to discuss. However, this does not fully achieve the goals of coming up with a complete concept that can be reflected in a thesis statement. Ask yourself a few questions about the audience to clarify behavioral purpose and objectives:

- How much does my audience already know about this topic?

- Where does my audience stand in its personal position on this topic?

- How far can I push my audience's perspectives to change?

- How much evidence or supporting material do I have to fully explain my concept or convince audience members of my position on the issue?

Being able to fully formulate a purpose is the first step in crafting a thesis statement that we will discuss in the next chapter. It is impossible to clarify the overall goals and concepts of a presentation without identifying the general, specific, and behavioral purposes – the complete purpose – at the beginning of the process of crafting the presentation. Having a clear purpose for your presentation will help you stay on track to narrow your focus during the research process leading to gratitude from your audience as they will understand your overall goals for them as they listen to your presentation as well. The goal is to start going somewhere, rather than nowhere.

7 Choosing a Topic and Building a Thesis

> **"If you don't know what you want to achieve in your presentation, your audience never will."**
>
> *—Harvey Diamond*

Choosing a topic should be the easiest part of a presentation; however, it can be so difficult if specific parameters are not given to the presenter to follow – which is what happens in most cases. How does a presenter choose a topic that is relevant and still interesting to themselves? The answer is to consider three elements: *Their personal passions, the audience's interests, and the presentation situation.* If a presenter asks important questions related to these three elements, they will have a well-rounded presentation that they will enjoy deliver and the audience will enjoy hearing.

Presenter's Passions

English Author and speaker, Nicholas Boothman says, "It's much easier to be convincing if you care about your topic. Figure out what's important to you about your message and speak from the heart." Searching the internet for top news and choosing a topic at random will not ensure that you deliver a topic you care about. This can damage your delivery because you will not display passion. Passion is the most important thing needed to make an impact with your speech and convince listeners to care along with you. Looking at your life and using that to guide you in finding a current issue or event that resonates with you is the most important part of choosing a topic. The first step in determining topics you are passionate about is to ask yourself, "What do I care about?" "What is important to me?" "Why do I care about this?" If this still does not help bring a topic to mind, consider current events or content that you may have recently researched, maybe something trending in the news you may have recently found yourself looking into further than the brief glimpse on a newsfeed (Fig. 7.1). Still not sure? Consider activities or hobbies you participate in and use that to lead you to a possible topic.

Audiences Interests

AT&T presentation research manager Ken Haemer is credited with saying, "Designing a presentation without an audience in mind is like writing a love letter and addressing it: To Whom It May Concern." This is quite accurate when it comes to topic selection.

© By Tero Vesalainen/Shutterstock.com

Fig 7.1 Avoid just randomly picking news topics. Use the current events you see happening to find a concept or topic you are passionate about.

Source: https://www.shutterstock.com/image-photo/online-news-mobile-phone-close-smartphone-1204164946

Every audience is different and understanding who is in the room will help the presenter choose a topic that not only appeals to themselves but also addresses the concerns of the people in the room. How does a presenter identify the audience and their interests? Asking questions again is the best practice in this situation. Ask, "Who is in the room?" Consider demographic information including genders, ages, ethnicities, and religious or political affiliations. This not only helps build content that is relevant to the people who will listen but will help you narrow down a specific area within that topic you will discuss. Ask, "What information is important to this particular group of people?" The audience will influence the information you share. Examples, stories, and even data you include must resonate with the audience. For example, if an audience is comprised of all college-aged students from 18 to 21, with a blend of genders, cultural backgrounds, and even political convictions, then it would be inappropriate to share parenting examples or discuss topics relevant to only women or only to men.

The last question and possibly the most important question you could ask is "What could save their lives?" A little dramatic yes, but everyone has a current problem or need that your presentation could resolve. Considering how you would feel as an audience member or what you might want to know if you attended a presentation about your topic is a great way to narrow down the exact focus for your presentation. As a presenter, recalling past experiences of listening to disappointing or impactful speeches will help you remember the importance of considering the audience when building your topic.

The Situation

Why were you asked to speak? What is the event or the occasion? Knowing details about what you are speaking for will also help you tailor the content. The topic must be appropriate for the situation. For example, if a presenter is asked to speak at a graduation ceremony, the occasion calls for celebrating the future, moving forward, becoming who you are meant to be, the topic must address that tone of the event. The graduation ceremony is not a time to sell goods or talk about yourself and your personal success.

Building a Topic

The Scenario: You are asked to present a speech at a conference for users of a software product. You have only used the software for a year and had previously attended the conference shortly after starting to use the program. The first year you attended, you had a difficult time finding presentations that taught you the basics and helped you improve the user experience. In order to present you must submit a topic for approval, considering your personal passion, the audience's interests, and the situation how do you come up with a topic?

Your Passion: Your main use of the software is building and sending timed communications to email customers. You recall your frustration as a new user not being able to learn some of those basic skills that would have made your job easier at the last conference and see it as a valuable tool for all users. You decide that you want to teach people the basics using the software because that is what you do the most and are wanting to help others with this knowledge. But what basics should you teach?

The Audience's Interests: Who is in the room? Reflecting on your experience, you come up with a list of common traits for your audience: all members use the software, all members use it for communications, all members have the same type of customer, and all members have a varied knowledge and comfort level of technology. Considering the audience's interests beyond their traits (and also in this case, possibly your own in the past) will help narrow down the best concepts to teach.

The Situation: The situation is the user conference itself. The conference is held to inform and display the variety of uses for the technology and focuses on users helping users. The situation requires that you inform and teach other users and you share about the technological product utilizing a demonstration.

Result: By reflecting on the core uses of the software, considering what you love most is using the program for communications, remembering that the audience wants to know basic uses of the software and how to implement those uses into their job, all while set against the backdrop of the conference and its purpose will help you develop the best topic. As a result, you decide that teaching how to create a communication plan and delivering the steps to time email delivery is something that would be beneficial, especially for the variety of people and backgrounds in the room.

Now that you know how to arrive at a topic idea, how do you put it into words? Creating a thesis statement is the best way to submit a topic so that event organizers or professors know what to expect when you arrive at your podium, prepared to present.

The Thesis Statement

As you step onto the elevator after a long meeting, you happen to look up and lock eyes with your boss. She asks about the meeting you just attended, and you know she only has about 1 minute until she has to walk off to another appointment. What would you say? How does someone summarize an hour-long meeting into a short 1-minute statement? Easy… or maybe not. This example is called the elevator test (Fig. 7.2). Many individuals struggle to be able to summarize something like a meeting or even a presentation in a short and simple summary. Considering an elevator pitch moment like the one here is helpful and emphasizes the importance of a short and simple statement for their thesis that still can accomplish a clear description of the presentation. A single statement that clearly covers every aspect of a presentation often seems to be one of the hardest parts of crafting a presentation; however if a presenter can do this, they will be clearer and more concise when creating the full presentation and will gain appreciation from the audience for their simple communication of their ideas.

Building a Thesis

First, when building anything, one must *pull together all their materials*. In this case, the goals and purpose of speaking, the general topic at large, the lessons to be shared, and traits of the audience will be the elements needed to create a thesis statement.

© By Andrey_Popov/Shutterstock.com

Fig 7.2 Can you share your thesis in a minute or less? Using the Elevator pitch test is a good way to make sure your thesis is clear.

Source: https://www.shutterstock.com/image-photo/young-african-businesspeople-having-conversation-elevator-1516328099

The next step in the process is *organizing a structure.* The structure begins with the purpose, then the general topic, next how it solves a problem, or a lesson discussed, and lastly how it benefits the audience.

The last step in building this thesis is the *quality control assessment.* Can it hold up to the expectations of the situation? When someone builds a structure, there is always a test to make sure it is strong and stable; the same goes for a statement. Testing the thesis by asking qualifying questions to make sure it achieves the overall goals of the presenter, the audience, and the situation will expose weaknesses in the thesis or confirm the statement is sound and will be a perfect guide for creating the presentation.

Below is a scenario to work through using the steps for building an excellent thesis. Consider an upcoming presentation you may have and try this method.

The Scenario: A college professor assigns a presentation that requires a student to choose a current event or issue and present that current event or issue to the audience full of college students. This assignment is not very specific and is very open for a student to have flexibility in their choices for the presentation. The class policy is that only one student may present on a topic unless the two students discuss a different perspective about that current event or issue. Students A and B both choose to discuss current gun control policies in the United States as they start to build a thesis.

Pulling Together Materials: The students should list things they may want to discuss, such as the purpose, gun control policies to focus on, their personal opinion about gun control, the impact of gun violence on the audience (in this case, the audience would be fellow college students), and any other elements they to be included in the presentation.

Organizing Materials into a Structure: The assignment, while broad, can fit with an informative or persuasive purpose. Informing or persuading the class about gun control will be the lead in the thesis. Next in the structure, the presenter will state exactly what topic they will inform or persuade the audience about, in this case gun control policies. The policies they wish to discuss must be identified (current policies, specific gun types, old policies, all of these are options found in research and will be chosen based on the presenter's personal passion.) After stating the overall topic, the next element in the statement is the stance taken within the presentation and perhaps a lesson that will be conveyed. Lastly, they share how a specific audience is impacted by the topic shared.

From this list, and the overall content found in research, Student A creates this thesis: *I will inform the audience about the current gun control policies and how they encourage an increase in gun related violence among college students.*

Student B does not feel confident in thesis building. They also are not passionate about gun control, but they understand it is a debated topic in the news lately. Rather than following a systematic approach to build a thesis statement, they merely submit a topic. They choose to submit: *Gun Control Policies.* While this may be their topic, the professor will have difficulty understanding the perspective they will present and if it is different from Student A because this is not a clear thesis statement. The problem with this submission first and foremost is that it is not a sentence or even a statement. Second, there is no *quality control assessment* of what they will discuss about gun control. Is it good or bad? Who is affected? How are they affected? How does this matter to college students? What purpose are they pursuing? Will the audience be persuaded or informed or entertained? Student B will not have their topic approved and will have to try again because they have not done a quality assessment.

You can see how using the build approach (Fig. 7.3) will help any presenter consider all the important factors to include in order to develop an articulate thesis statement. In return, clarity from the thesis will guide the presenter as they begin to craft content to share and help them more effectively cut excessive or irrelevant details. As presenters begin to research and organize material they want to share, the thesis will be the measuring device that qualifies all of the supporting material and sources used in the final presentation.

"If you can't write your message in a sentence, you can't say it in an hour." Author and communication expert Dianna Booher gives us this wisdom when considering our topic and our thesis. Do not give little attention to the steps in the process of building a thesis. Asking qualifying questions at every step of the topic and thesis development processes will ensure a clear, concise, and articulate message from the beginning.

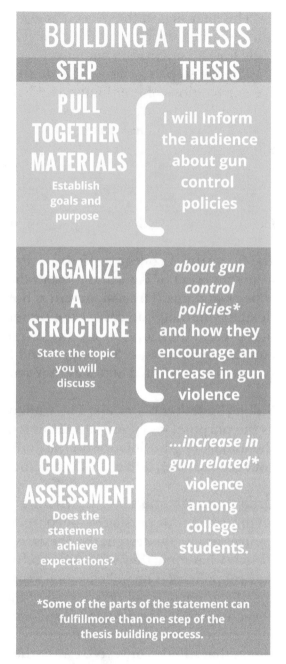

Fig 7.3 Follow the build approach to get a clear and concise thesis statement.

Source: Amanda Gilliland

References

Nicholas Boothman. AZQuotes.com, Wind and Fly LTD, 2021. https://www.azquotes.com/author/41494-Nicholas_Boothman, accessed January 29, 2021.

TAKE ACTION

Coming up with a topic can be challenging. Use the following steps when you have an upcoming presentation to help you determine both a topic and craft the thesis statement for your presentation.

1. What are things you are interested in? What is a current event or topic that you have recently researched further online? What is an activity that you participate in? List them here:

    _____

    _____

2. What is the demographic makeup of your audience?

    _____

    _____

3. What are some things the audience have in common?

    _____

    _____

4. Why should the audience care about the topic you are interested in? How can they benefit from knowing the information you are sharing? How could it save their lives?

    _____

    _____

5. What is the reason you were asked to speak? Was it a class assignment? What is the requirement of the class assignment? Was it an event? What is the purpose of the event?

    _____

Have you ever sat down to watch the national anthem during the Super Bowl? It is one of the most difficult but the most loved songs to perform and the Super Bowl is a massive stage to perform it on (Fig. 8.1) Often, when someone starts out singing very strong, it creates excitement for the audience watching the performance. However, as the song reaches the end, what if the performer hits a very bad note right as they conclude? In this scenario, the audience will walk away thinking about how the song was terribly performed. How could this be? Every note was perfect except for the last. How could an audience think the whole song was bad when only one note was sung wrong? Likewise, when someone stands up to the microphone to sing the national anthem and starts off very badly, the audience's perspective of them will immediately be negative. Maybe the singer recovers and ends the song perfectly, but the damage is done. The audience started off hearing negative tones and held that against the singer through the entire song making them walk away saying it was terrible. The same goes for introductions and conclusions. The introduction and conclusion of a presentation must be the strongest points in the delivery of a presentation, otherwise the audience will not listen or will walk away feeling dissatisfied at the end. This idea is called the *Primacy/Recency Effect*.

Fig 8.1 Every performance requires a strong beginning and end to ensure the audience has a positive reaction.

Source: https://www.shutterstock.com/image-photo/boca-raton-floridausa-december-07-2019-1582103257

The Primacy/Recency Effect Is the concept that an audience will remember the first and the last things they hear most above all other information they are given. This is why your introduction and your conclusion must shine when presenting, because the audience will remember them the most and reflect on your presentation based on how you made them feel during these two portions of the presentation (Morrison, 2015).

Introduction Statement

The introduction is the most important part of the presentation. Starting off strong will ensure the audience will continue listening, and grabbing their attention will make them eager to hear what you have to say next. This is why a presenter should spend quality time crafting an introduction statement so it will shine above all other content. Looking at the introduction as something needed to be built, you can pull together the different elements required to make a quality statement to start off the speech. So, what are these components? The introduction includes an *attention getting device (AGD), orienting material, striking statement,* and finally a *preview statement* sharing the three main points of the presentation.

Attention Getting Device

The beginning of a presentation should always start with an AGD. An AGD does not include "um..." or "good morning" or "my speech is about..." Many presenters start off with these contrite or overused phrases because they are uncomfortable and have not put effort into an introduction statement with a strong AGD. What is an AGD? This is the megaphone that makes the audience sit up and really begin actively listening to you (Fig. 8.2). An AGD can be stories, humorous statements, rhetorical questions, suspense,

© By Gearstd/Shutterstock.com

Fig 8.2 The attention getting device is like the megaphone that gains the audience's attention at the beginning of the presentation.

Source: https://www.shutterstock.com/image-illustration/3d-rendering-white-blue-portable-cordless-1204753960

quotes, or even surprising statistics or facts that will set up the presentation and grab the audience's attention immediately.

Types of AGDs

Stories show vulnerability, make the audience comfortable with the presenter, or set up a concept that may be unfamiliar in a more familiar setting. Stories can be personal, or they can be about others as long as it's relevant to the topic and is brief in detail. A story used during the introduction should be short but easy to understand and still make sense in relation to the rest of the topic.

Humorous statements are always welcome to an audience. Starting off with a laugh will make people comfortable and show that you are easy going. If you decide to use humor, make sure it is something that you typically use in your everyday life. Some people may not consider themselves humorous and those people should not be telling jokes in front of an audience because it is not something that they are comfortable doing. If you enjoy being humorous and it is something you are comfortable with, make sure that you evaluate the type of humor you are using based on who is in the audience. Consider this question, "would my family be embarrassed by the type of humor I am using?" If the answer potentially could be no or you are unsure, then you may need to consider an alternative humorous story or joke or consider leaving humor out completely.

During the 2018 White House Correspondent's Dinner, the invited comedian, Michelle Wolf, may have allowed her comedy to go too far and potentially change the course of the history of the event. Wolf, known for her vulgar and barbed comedy, did what she normally does in a comedy routine; however, the situation and the mixed political perspectives in the audience at the dinner called for a more refined and lighthearted poking of fun rather than comedy that goes for the jugular. By the end of the event, she had offended many people including the very person she made jokes about, White House Press Secretary Sarah Huckabee Sanders. In the following weeks she faced a mix of criticism and praise from a variety of different sources; however, the audience as a whole did not walk away from her presentation feeling like it was successful. The mixed reviews indicate that the direction she took her comedy was not appropriate for the event or the audience and limited her ability to impact people in that moment. Because of her choices, organizers of the event considered completely changing the format for future events because of the backlash, and television networks have considered not airing the event in the future (Grynbaum, 2018).

Rhetorical questions are questions that the presenter does not want to be answered out loud. Asking a rhetorical question is an excellent way to get the audience thinking about your topic immediately. For example, if you did a presentation with the goal of encouraging people to stop or avoid using e-cigarettes, you might start with this rhetorical question: "What if I told you there was a way for you to immediately improve your health and limit your risk of lung cancer?" This rhetorical question would probably trigger the immediate subconscious response from audience members of "yes!" everyone wants to be healthier everyone wants to avoid lung cancer if they can, and so this question prepares them to hear solutions to be healthier and prevent lung cancer related to e-cigarette use.

Suspense can take many forms. It can be used with statistics or facts, in the form of a rhetorical question, or even with a quote. Suspense while not limited to questions or stories is a tactic that helps keep the audience engaged throughout the presentation. Suspense will open up the audience's curiosity and leave them with the unspoken requirement of sitting through the rest of the presentation to find out what happens next. Typically, suspense is set up in a story format, however, as described earlier, can be utilized with many different types of AGDs.

Quotes are an excellent way to utilize an outside source to build credibility regarding your topic and purpose. Often, quotes are inspiring or challenging and have survived the test of time making them a reliable way to engage an audience. if you were presenting an entertaining speech with the goal of inspiring your audience to never give up in the face of adversity, you may use the 1941 quote from Winston Churchill, "This is the lesson: never give in, never give in, never, never, never, never—in nothing, great or small, large or petty—never give in except to convictions of honour and good sense." Walking up to a podium and having these be your first words will instantly set the tone of inspiration and determination that you want for this type of presentation.

Surprising statistics or facts can be used to defuse controversial topics from the very beginning of a presentation. Utilizing research first thing will demonstrate your credibility and integrity. Oftentimes, when faced with specific facts or statistics that may not be widely spread in the mainstream media, audiences will become more open to hearing content about a topic that they may have positions or opinions already formed about. If your purpose for presenting is persuasion, you would want to utilize statistics and facts at the very beginning to get people listening. For example, if your presentation was to influence the audience to take mental health seriously and remove the stigma that it is very limited in the amount of people it affects, you might present this attention getting statement: "In 2018, the National College health assessment report stated that 63% of college students who responded to their research, were affected by anxiety. This clearly indicates that anxiety and mental health issues among college students is more widely common than many of us think or talk about" (Leblanc, 2019). Utilizing research makes it difficult for people in the audience who have never researched the topic and typically rely on their personal opinions to turn a deaf ear on your presentation after hearing valid research first thing.

Orienting Material

After opening with your AGD, the next step is to provide orienting material. This is a very important step in the introduction as it provides clarifying information regarding the topic. A presenter should not assume that the people in the audience know exactly what they are talking about and fail to provide important detail. This is a lot like when a person starts a story in the middle rather than at the beginning. When someone delivers information in this manner it is very confusing, and the listener feels behind through the entire conversation. Likewise, failing to include orienting material in your introduction will make your audience feel behind or lost. Even when the concept is simple or what the presenter would consider commonly known, that should not discourage them from including orienting material to clarify the topic they will be discussing. An attention getter without a follow-up statement clarifying the direction the speech will follow leaves the audience confused.

For example, if you were to use the attention getting quote from Winston Churchill that we used earlier and then went straight into your thesis without clarifying why you are sharing a quote that says to never give in, the introduction will lose some of its effectiveness.

Striking Statement

The striking statement that follows the orienting material often provides a promise or a challenge to the audience as a result of their listening or following the concepts provided in the presentation. For example, after sharing the statistic about anxiety in college students and sharing some orienting material that may discuss the importance of removing the stigma of mental health, a striking statement could be something like, "by the end of this presentation, you will know more about the very common issue of mental health and how to address it." The striking statement can be its own individual phrase, or it could be something within the thesis statement. Regardless of how it is stated, a striking statement is very important to create excitement and anticipation within the audience for the potential benefits that will come from listening to the presentation.

Wrapping up the Introduction

After building a unique AGD, clarifying information with orienting material, and providing a striking statement, the last elements of an introduction are a thesis statement and the preview of the presentation's three main points. The thesis statement may be combined within the striking statement or part of the orienting material. The key with the thesis statement is that it must be stated somewhere in the introduction after the AGD. While there isn't a specific rule for where the thesis may go, the presentation preview must be the last thing stated in the introduction. The preview sets up the body of the presentation and must not be placed earlier in the introduction or will not make sense.

Conclusion Statement

The conclusion is just as important as the introduction as we have learned through the primacy and recency effect. The goal is to end the presentation on a very high note and make it very clear that the presentation has come to an end. We've all sat in that audience where there's awkward silence or no one knows for sure if the speech is over and they should clap. A strong conclusion will ensure that the audience knows you are finished and know that it is time to provide you with applause.

Many presenters struggle with crafting a good strong conclusion. There's a level of comfort in saying things like "I'm done." Or using the *Looney Tunes* approach to your ending with "That's all folks!" (Fig. 8.3) or channeling your inner

Fig 8.3 The ending needs to be more than a Looney Toons ending. Avoid the temptation to say, "That's all folks!" at the end.

Source: https://www.shutterstock.com/image-photo/united-states-america-circa-2001-stamp-357586526

© By tristan tan/Shutterstock.com

Forrest Gump with an ending of "That's all I have to say about that." Find a way to have an eloquent statement that indicates you are finished talking rather than a verbal version of a walk off.

The elements included in a conclusion are the *review statement, the thesis, a clincher, and coming full circle back to the AGD*. The review statement is similar to the preview and must be stated first in the conclusion because it reviews the three main points that have been covered and wraps up the body of the speech.

Clincher

The clincher is the conclusion's version of an AGD. The clincher often will have a call to action, a challenge, or a reference back to the striking statement. The overall goal of including a clincher is to push the audience toward changing an attitude action or belief or reiterate what they just learned after listening to the presentation.

Coming Full Circle

One way to ensure that it is clear you are finished is to come full circle and state some of the things you said in your introduction. For example, in a presentation regarding mental health and college students, a conclusion may come full circle by stating the statistic used in the AGD (Fig. 8.4). This closing statement say something like, "follow the lead of the

© By Krisztian/Shutterstock.com

Fig 8.4 Work to come full circle with your conclusion by stating something you shared in the beginning of the presentation.

Source: https://www.shutterstock.com/image-vector/white-circle-arrows-on-blue-round-382329085

63% of students who say they have dealt with anxiety. The first step to resolving mental health issues is to admit you have something going on." This sentence clearly indicates the presentation is complete. It comes full circle stating the same statistic as the introduction. It also can be considered a clincher as it challenges the audience to take a specific action.

Structuring an introduction and conclusion in a way that makes sense to the audience and provides clarity for the issue at hand is important. No matter the presentation content or topic, it is always necessary to open and close strong in order to grab the audience's attention and keep them listening throughout the presentation. Work to ensure your introduction and conclusion shine.

References

Churchill, Winston, and Charles Eade. *The Unrelenting Struggle: War Speeches.* Cassell and Company, Ltd., 1942.

Grynbaum, Michael. "Did Michelle Wolf Kill the White House Correspondents' Dinner?" *The New York Times.* April 30, 2018. https://www.nytimes.com/2018/04/30/business/media/michelle-wolf-white-house-correspondents-dinner.html.

Morrison, Mike. "Primacy and Recency Effects in Learning." RapidBI. March 13, 2015. https://rapidbi.com/primacy-and-recency-effects-in-learning

TAKE ACTION

1. **Scenario:** You've been assigned a presentation discussing your local town's best eateries. Craft an AGD for a presentation recommending the best places to eat in your town.

_____

_____

_____

2. What type of AGD did you decide to use? _____

3. Now write a statement of orienting material. This should include the town you are discussing, the types of eateries you have chosen, and maybe some elements you utilized to choose those eateries (i.e., quality of food, atmosphere, or price)_____

_____

_____

_____

4. What is a striking statement you would use to create a challenge, promise something, or inspire the audience with for this introduction? Write it here. _____

_____

_____

Put it all together and you have a strong introduction statement to pair with your thesis and your preview statement. Write the completed introduction here:

_____

_____

_____

9 Presentation Cues

"Good transitions can make a speech more important to the audience because they feel they are being taken to a positive conclusion without having to travel a bumpy road."

—Joe Griffith

A bumpy road. This is exactly how the audience can feel without strong verbal presentation cues, thrown from side to side, bouncing from topic to topic. Each listener will be frustrated if verbal presentation cues are not included in a presentation. Why is this? While a presenter has a well-organized outline that they are able to follow, the audience does not. This is why verbally communicating the structure of your presentation as you work through the content point by point will help the audience be more comfortable while listening. Likewise, failure to communicate the structure by utilizing elements such as *a preview, a review, and transitions* will cause the audience to be frustrated, losing their interest or leaving them completely confused as you move through the content you want to share (Fig. 9.1).

© By Giedrius Akelis/Shutterstock.com

Fig 9.1 A winding bumpy road will make it difficult for a passenger. In the same way a speech without presentation cues will make an audience miserable.

Source: https://www.shutterstock.com/image-photo/bumpy-curvy-road-surrounded-by-labanoras-1553025662

A Smoother Journey

Presentation cues – *the preview, the review, and transitions* – are simple to create and provide a guide to what the audience will learn about or hear during the speech. Implementing presentation cues during a presentation is similar to utilizing a GPS while traveling. The destination we type in is the *thesis statement*; this prompts a route and list of directions to come on the screen. This route and direction list would be *the preview and the review*. As you travel through your presentation, *the transitions* are like the voice that comes on a short distance before each turn. Conversely, if we begin to travel without any travel aid, our passengers will feel every bump throughout the presentation. So how does the smooth ride versus the bumpy ride look in a presentation?

Gathering Content

Prior to creating these presentation cues, you must gather your content. We will discuss research and creating main points in further detail in future chapters; however, it is important for you to understand that to create cues, the research and main points must be completed. Furthermore, you must have a consistent *reason behind choosing the main points* that you share in order to create the different types of verbal cues.

For example, let's say you own a business called Touch of Home Bakery, and the Chamber of Commerce in your area asks you to do an informative presentation on the best desserts offered at your bakery. This is where the reasoning behind choosing specific main points comes in. First, you consider what desserts are your favorite, then you consider which desserts are best sellers, and which are typically left over at the end of each day. Utilizing these different attributes, you evaluate each dessert in your bakery and come up with your three best desserts offered: red velvet cake, sweet potato pie, and banana pudding. Using the reasoning behind choosing these desserts becomes the building blocks for the cues in a way that it makes sense to the audience (Fig. 9.2).

© By morrowlight/Shutterstock.com

Fig 9.2 Even a speech about a bakery needs clear presentation cues. These will keep things on track and maybe gain your business support and a following.

Source: https://www.shutterstock.com/image-photo/woman-making-creamy-top-cupcakes-closeup-444500605

The Preview Statement

The preview statement is essentially a list of each individual main point you plan to share with the audience during your presentation. Each main point must have a strong, simple label to help the audience recall the information after the presentation is over. For example, with our bakery presentation, the labels of red velvet cake, sweet potato pie, and banana pudding, all have simple labels. However if you were to over-complicate these labels by saying *red velvet cake covered in cream cheese, banana pudding utilizing shortbread cookies, or sweet potato pie freshly baked each day,* it would be a little too wordy and offer details that are unnecessary to share in the preview.

The preview is stated after the introduction and the thesis statement. An appropriate thesis statement combined with a preview for our bakery presentation would be as follows: *the three best desserts at the touch of home bakery are red velvet cake, sweet potato pie, and banana pudding.* This simple thesis and preview statement make it very clear to the audience that they will hear about these three main topics related to the thesis of best desserts at your bakery.

The important thing to remember about including a preview statement is that it is very helpful for the audience to follow along with what is coming up in the presentation. Have you ever attended a banquet or an event that had a program and immediately sat down and looked at the order of the agenda? Or more specifically, the last item on that agenda? A preview statement provides guidance just like this. The audience know exactly what you will cover, and exactly which point is last in the presentation. The preview statement keeps them from guessing about content and how long the presentation will last. While we never want people to hope our presentation is over, it gives listeners peace of mind to understand the exact order of the speech so that way they can stay engaged and connected. It is only natural for people to want to know the order of events and providing that in a presentation will allow them to have some gratitude toward you as a presenter for sharing those details.

The Review Statement

The review statement is found directly after the body of the presentation. After you finish your final main point, you would share your simple labels again much like you did in the preview statement. The review statement for your bakery presentation would be something like this: *Today I have shared with you our bakery's best items: red velvet cake, sweet potato pie, and banana pudding.* While this is a very simple element, it is something that we often overlook because we are eager to get to the conclusion of the presentation. Having a review statement allows the audience to settle in for the last words of your presentation. If they are unaware that you are shifting gears to a conclusion, they may think you are still talking about another main point.

The review statement is essential as this allows the audience to remember the three things that you felt were the most important to share about your topic. Remember, they do not have a copy of your notes in front of them so having a summary of content to help them recall the information you shared is vital to your presentation's success and longevity in the minds of your audience.

Transitions

As previously mentioned in our GPS example, transitions are often like that calming voice telling you that in half a mile you're about to turn. Transitions are essential to a presentation's success because if an audience cannot stay engaged with what you are saying they could become confused about which point you were discussing, or they could stop listening, or spend the remainder of your presentation frustrated because they are lost.

Each transition includes three basic elements: *an internal review, a connection, and an internal preview.* Each element does not have to have its own individual sentence; however, the phrasing and statement you use as your transition must show a strong internal review, connection, and internal preview. Let's evaluate each element using our touch of home bakery presentation example and transitioning from point (1) Red velvet cake into point (2) Sweet potato pie:

Internal review: *Red velvet cake is one of our most popular desserts.*

Connection: *However, you may be more of a pie lover instead of cake!*

Internal preview: *Well, you are in luck, because the next dessert I want to share about is sweet potato pie – our second most popular dessert!*

As you can see, it does not require three full sentences to include each individual element required for a transition. As long as each element is included and the reasoning behind the order of your points is shared (in this case, it is because pie is the second most popular dessert based on your research), then the audience will be able to take a smoother turn into the new talking point.

This three-part transition works between your first two points and your last two points. However, it will look a little different prior to your first main point. You see, you must still transition from your preview statement into your first main point. However, there is no previous point to review, so in this case, you would only include a connection statement *clarifying why this point has been chosen first,* followed by an internal preview of that point. For example, in our bakery presentation the first transition into Red Velvet Cake may look something like this:

Connection: *We will start with the bestselling dessert on our menu.*

Internal preview: *It happens to be one of my favorite desserts and seems to be the favorite of most of our customers, red velvet cake.*

As you can see while this transition is a little bit different it still smoothly steers the listeners to focus on the very first main point. This is important because the discussion of main points is very different from the attention-grabbing introduction and a transition allows the audience to prepare to listen to something that may sound a little bit different.

Arriving Safely

Utilizing verbal presentation cues helps the audience stay the course with the presenter in a way that it allows them to be engaged and impacted by your content. The whole goal throughout the presentation from the introduction to the conclusion is to utilize elements like the preview, transitions, and review in order to help the audience arrive at each main checkpoint of the journey you take them on.

TAKE ACTION

1. You are assigned a presentation to discuss the best places to live in your town. List three main points you would include in a speech below in the order you will use:

   _____   _____   _____

2. Why did you organize the points in this order? What was the reason?

   _____

3. Craft a preview statement using the points you created: _____

   _____

4. Create a transition sentence connecting point 1 and point 2 below:

   _____

   _____

5. Create a transition sentence connecting points 2 and 3 below:

   _____

   _____

6. Create a review statement using the points you created:

   _____

10 | Research

"Research is formalized curiosity. It is poking and prying with a purpose."

—Zora Neale Hurston

Research can be considered the unsexy work involved in creating a presentation while, at the same time, a necessary step in building credibility and making a presentation noteworthy. Research is not something that everyone is passionate about doing. It feels like an overwhelming task that can often come across as unenjoyable. However, *if a presenter is choosing to discuss something they are passionate about, the process of research should be a joy not a burden.*

Did you know that research happens every day in everyone's lives? Consider your use of social media. Facts and examples and stories are shared by people online and one of those may pique your interest. What Happens next? Most of us dig deeper into the issues or facts shared online by those we are connected with. This in itself is research. Research is simply *the process of finding more information about a specific topic.*

For those of us who may not be in a field that regularly does research, the idea of having to research for a presentation can often be overwhelming. It is best to break it into steps to avoid burnout. *Early research, detailed research, evaluation, and building credibility* are the steps you can take to ensure the research process is enjoyable as well as creates credibility and interest for your presentation.

Early Research

The first step when you sit down to do your research should be a basic early search. The best place to start when researching any topic is a search engine online. Google and Bing are two of the top search engines available to the general public online. During your early search, set a timer for 20–30 minutes and do a general search regarding your topic. During this search, bookmark articles that look relevant, take notes of authors or sites and publications that have consistent information regarding the topic, and take note of keywords and topics that you are seeing within the articles and the information you find online. Once time is up, review the topics and keywords to see if there are any trending themes. This search not only will give you these small details that help create a more specific search in future steps but also will tell you what kind of information is available to you regarding your topic at large (Fig. 10.1).

© By PK Studio/Shutterstock.com

Fig 10.1 Using a search engine is the best way to kick off your research efforts.

Source: https://www.shutterstock.com/image-photo/bangkok-thailand-january-24-2016-woman-565063075

For example, you are assigned a topic to research about the U.S. Immigration policy. You notice the search brings back many sites that end with .org or .gov. You note terms found including citizenship, deportation, visas, refugees, asylees, naturalization, and green card. Themes you are seeing include DREAMer program, policy changes, and asylum programs. You may see names like President Barack Obama, President Donald Trump, and President Joe Biden.

Detailed Research

The next step would be a more detailed search utilizing the keywords, terms, authors, publications, and themes you have found in your *early research*. Your research may show positives or negatives specifically related to your topic. You may have seen themes or specific programs and policies that you want to learn more about so narrowing your search down to specifics rather than broad terms will help you gain more detailed information and excellent sources for supporting material.

One way to make sure your research is more specific is to consider utilizing advanced search options in your search engine. Maybe your topic is about current immigration policies. If that is the case, you might select a time period of the last 12 months or even a little shorter depending on the topic. As we found in the early research phase, many websites that discuss immigration policy from a non-partisan perspective are going to have a .org or .gov web address. Advanced searches can limit your search results to those specific addresses.

Evaluation and Building Credibility

Once you've gone through your detailed research to pull articles and information that will help you build your presentation, evaluate the quality of your content. The audience will appreciate supporting material you find in your research as long as the source can be considered an expert on the topic or be related to the topic in some way.

For example, if you are presenting a new topic regarding skincare, you might want to share a quote you find from Us Weekly provided by Jessica Alba. At first glance, utilizing the opinion of an actress may not be deemed credible to the audience or the topic itself. This is where evaluation and building credibility come into play. Many audiences may only know about Jessica's acting career. However, when you share the fact that Jessica Alba has designed a skincare line complete with makeup and even baby skincare products, she becomes more credible to the subject matter. Looking at the source and determining if they are considered experts on the material is part of the evaluation process. Next, building credibility is about framing the information in a way that it gives background information on that source. We see this in our Jessica Alba example. Mentioning her skincare experience as well as her business ventures focused on skincare during the presentation will help build credibility for a quote from her more so than if you just mention that she is an actress.

Other Resources

Utilizing online search engines is not the only place to research and find supporting material. Online search engines are the beginning of the process and can lead to unexpected places and information that you would have never found had you merely shared information you already knew in a presentation. Consider utilizing libraries in your area in order to research beyond the normal search engine. Many libraries have databases with academic and scholarly research that can provide some really strong supporting material for your presentation and build your credibility. Librarians also are experts in research and can help you format your search criteria to get the most out of your searches.

Qualifying Research

Once you retrieve all of the information you wish to utilize in your presentation, it is very important to evaluate each source and determine if it is relevant and necessary to include in your final presentation. Being very picky about what you include will make sure that you are being intentional about the information that you wish to share with the audience making it the best presentation it could be.

Ask yourself if the audience will trust the sources you have chosen. If the answer is no, consider looking for other sources. Sources like Wikipedia can direct you to reliable sources; however, Wikipedia is not considered a reliable source to support your research. So, as you find information, evaluate the sources to ensure your credibility is intact. Maybe you believe your source is a valid one. Consider framing or justifying the use of that particular source. Maybe you are sharing a quote from professional American basketball

© By lev radin/Shutterstock.com

Fig 10.2 Remember to share specific details about a source to ensure your audience accepts it as credible.

Source: https://www.shutterstock.com/image-photo/new-york-ny-june-26-2018-1121462966

player Shaquille O'Neal that is about business and leadership. Your audience may not believe that he is the best or most credible resource to discuss business and leadership. However, if you introduce the information by first sharing that Shaquille O'Neal not only is a basketball player but also holds a doctorate degree in human resource development, the audience would be more willing to accept the quote from him as a credible source (Fig. 10.2).

No matter the subject matter, research will always help boost your credibility and give you exceptional supporting material for your presentation. Do not put off the research, find a topic you are passionate about, and use as much information to be considered credible and trustworthy as you deliver your presentation.

11 Types of Supporting Material and Sources

The process of research that you learned about in Chapter 10 is a lot like mining for gems. All of the gold nuggets and jewels that you would find are a lot like the different types of supporting material that you can utilize in your speech. The various mines that you do the digging in are like your sources for those types of supporting material. All of this is found in the overall process of research. Now that you've successfully done the research, you have a handful of sources and types of supporting material to include in your presentation. Supporting material from credible sources will elevate the value and credibility of any presentation.

There are various types of supporting material that can be used in a presentation. These include *facts, statistics, examples, stories, narratives, comparison, contrast,* and *testimony.* Supporting material can be found in a variety of sources during the process of research. Sources can include *books, academic journals, Internet sources, magazines, newspapers,* and *through citation chasing.*

Types of Supporting Material

Oxford Languages Dictionary (2021) defines *Fact* as a thing that is known to be true especially when it can be proved. Facts can be verified. Here are some simple facts about the United States of America: *there are 50 states that comprise the United States of America,* or *Joe Biden is America's 46th president,* or *Alaska is the largest state in the union.* These three statements are verifiable pieces of information that cannot be refuted which is what qualifies them as fact.

Statistics are numerical facts gathered through the process of scientific research applied to a specific sample. Statistics should not be utilized as fact. They should be utilized as support for a hypothesis or opinion shared in a presentation. Statistics are not absolute data. Because they are gathered from a sample, we cannot utilize statistics as a final truth about a specific topic or group of people (Fig. 11.1).

For example, the American Psychological Association reported results from their 2013 survey of college counseling centers that 41.6% of college students have Anxiety as their top mental health concern. While this statistic is helpful in understanding that anxiety is a real issue for college students, it should not be presented as an absolute number used to represent the entire population of college students. Why? First, if you are presenting about this topic today, in the year 2021, this survey has data that is 8 years old. This means the group of college students and the cultural environment in which the survey was completed are not quite identical to today, meaning the response numbers could have changed. Second, not every college campus has a counseling center, which means some campuses

Fig 11.1 Using statistical data to indicate trends is an excellent way to support your points.

Source: https://www.shutterstock.com/image-photo/silhouette-cropped-shot-businessman-hand-working-385335934

are not accounted for in the overall research results. Third, responses to surveys are a sample of the general population being researched. Without 100% participation from all colleges and students on their campuses, we cannot verify that 41.6% of students are concerned about anxiety. However, utilizing the survey as an indication of a trend provides support for the hypothesis that many college students are concerned about anxiety without falsely stating numbers as fact. Here's an example of the wrong and right ways to use this statistic as supporting material:

WRONG: *41.6% of **all college** students have anxiety at the top of their concerns.*

RIGHT: *According to this data, we can assume that anxiety is a really important issue that is on the minds of many college students.*

Examples used to support your presentation can be objects or facts used to explain something you are discussing. Oftentimes you need to utilize examples that are commonly understood by the general audience in order to make sense of things that are complicated or need clarification. In a situation where you are presenting about academic dishonesty, you may explain the example of plagiarizing a paper as one of many ways one could be found guilty of academic dishonesty.

Stories whether fiction or nonfiction are an engaging way to capture an audience's attention and help them understand the concept you may be discussing. You may utilize stories found in sources in your research or your own personal stories. If you share a story, make sure that you give enough detail to keep the audience on the same page as you without rambling. Your story should have a beginning, a middle, and an end, as well as details about the setting and the lead character.

Narratives are much like stories; however, they typically will be open ended. Narratives are excellent in the event you are presenting something persuasive or hope to influence an audience to take action.

Comparison and Contrast implemented in a presentation will provide an example of how something is similar or different to the concept that you are explaining. Let's say you are presenting about the effects of caffeine. You might want to compare putting gas in a car to consuming caffeine. Both are liquid substances that give energy to get going. On the other hand, you may want to use a contrasting example of a car's gas tank on empty being the opposite of how your body feels after consuming caffeine. Showing similarities or differences can help an audience make sense of a more complex issue when shared alongside a more commonly known concept.

"They say…." is becoming a common lead on most stories people share nowadays. "Who is they?" You make ask. In a presentation, we can share quotes from reliable sources in order to provide expert analysis, eyewitness accounts, or personally experienced information through the use of *testimony*. Testimony comes from people who have expertise on a subject or have personally lived through a concept you are explaining. Testimony is presented in the form of a quote from that source. The key in utilizing testimony is providing credential information about the source. For example, if you were to share testimony from Dr. Anthony Fauci regarding COVID-19, you would want to include details from his background that qualify him to speak about the virus. Rather than just stating that Dr. Fauci is an American Physician, you would also include that he has a background of being an immunologist and also is the director of the U.S. National Institute of Allergy and Infectious Diseases. All of these facets of his background increase his credibility to talk about an infectious disease more so than a general physician (Fig. 11.2).

© By Microgen/Shutterstock.com

Fig 11.2 Testimony is an excellent source of information that builds credibility for the speaker and trust from the audience.

Source: https://www.shutterstock.com/image-photo/media-interview-group-journalists-surrounding-vip-376505077

Sources of Supporting Material

Books are where it all starts. Books are consistently available as a source for information. Using library resources to access books and find content will provide you with supporting material like stories, examples, narratives, and testimony.

Newspapers provide daily articles about a topic and are an excellent source of testimony, stories, and examples. They also can be a good secondhand resource for finding primary research. The caution with using newspaper as a source is that because these are generated daily, information can change, grow, or be corrected. Be sure to frame the material gained from newspapers with dates and verify the information is current and as accurate as possible.

Magazines are like newspapers, covering current events with more in-depth coverage of an issue that is fully researched. Magazines give excellent examples, stories, narratives, testimony, and often will point to primary research.

Academic Journals are professional publications that publish doctoral and professional research. The research in an academic journal is evaluated by fellow researchers. Journals are an excellent source for facts, statistics, examples, and comparison and contrast.

Another source for finding research today is *the Internet*. Internet sources can vary in accuracy and credibility. It is important to evaluate web sites by looking for a publisher, author, and a publication date. Not all internet articles are created equal, and a presenter must be very selective of the information they choose to share. Using sites such as blogs and social media should be evaluated for credibility and used sparingly. These are excellent pages to find stories, examples, testimony, and even lead us to outside research.

Reference sites online such as Wikipedia are excellent sources to learn more about the topic; however, Wikipedia specifically should not be used as a primary source because much of the information is crowd sourced. You can use Wikipedia as well as other resources to find further sources through the practice of *Citation Chasing*. Citation Chasing is a practice of using reference lists to find further research on the subject. Wikipedia has hyperlinked references that you can use to cite and support your presentation content.

There is such a strong variety of Sources and Supporting Material in our world today compared to many years ago. Research is more accessible and provides more than we can ever include in our presentation. The key is finding a variety of material to show that you have done due diligence to support your topic and build your credibility.

References

"Fact." Accessed March 5, 2021. https://www.oxfordlearnersdictionaries.com/us/definition/english/fact?q=fact

"College Students' Mental Health Is a Growing Concern, Survey Finds." Monitor on Psychology. American Psychological Association, June 2013. https://www.apa.org/monitor/2013/06/college-students

"Anthony Fauci." Wikipedia. Wikimedia Foundation, March 1, 2021. https://en.wikipedia.org/wiki/Anthony_Fauci.

12 | Choosing Content

> "Ask yourself, 'If I had only sixty seconds on the stage, what would I absolutely have to say to get my message across?'"
>
> —*Jeff Dewar*

Choosing content can be overwhelming if you have not used the tips suggested for clarifying your thesis. Narrowing down the most important things to include is a skill necessary to ensure clarity for your message and for the audience. Identifying relevant content that achieves the goal is done by asking some important questions about your *purpose, your audience, and your own passion.*

Your Purpose

Remember the potential purposes your speech could achieve? The three purposes discussed in Chapter 6 were informative, persuasive, and inspirational; however, you could have additional goals for your presentation that you need to identify as you start to evaluate what content to include. If you plan to inform, you will need to find definitions or demonstrations that illustrate the concept and find statistical supporting material to support your position on the topic. If you plan to persuade you may want to consider benefits for the audience, explain why choosing your position would make their lives easier, and find supporting material like facts and testimony to include that will prove your personal position is the best position to have regarding the topic. Knowing your purpose can help you identify the right kinds of supporting material to support your argument and prove your position when discussing your topic.

The Audience

Many presenters only consider their own personal perspectives while overlooking the audience's interests. This is a misstep in the process of curating content. First and foremost, considering the audience's perspective will direct your research, help you select proper supporting materials, and consider examples that are relevant to them.

How do we evaluate an audience in a way that it helps us choose content? Asking good questions. A good presenter asks all kinds of questions to make sure the content is the best it can be. So, what questions do we ask about the audience? First, *who are they*?

Fig 12.1 It is important to identify who is in the room when you build your content.

Source: https://www.shutterstock.com/image-vector/human-resources-concept-target-market-audience-764492740

(Fig. 12.1). Who is sitting in the room? Consider the demographics – elements such as ethnicity, gender, and age. Consider other characteristics such as political affiliations, religious beliefs, professions or stages of life, and common interests. These will direct the content you choose to include. For example, if the whole room is full of college-aged students, with a mix of genders and ethnicities, various ages, with many different programs of study, then supporting material should be how it specifically impacts that general group of college students. You wouldn't want to discuss parenting or marriage-related examples with a room full of students who predominantly do not have kids or are not married. However, you may use examples related to student life or supporting material and research specifically aimed at that particular generation and specifically regarding those who attend college.

Once you identify who is in the room, you need to dig deeper into your topic of choice and ask yourself, *why should they care?* In his work, *The Rhetorical Situation (1968)*, Lloyd Bitzer shares, "In every rhetorical situation, there will be at least one controlling exigence which functions as the organizing principle: it specifies the audience to be addressed and the change to be affected." Exigence is a problem to resolve or a need to be addressed for a specific audience. So, ask yourself or even consider asking someone in the audience, "what is your problem?" Now, if you ask an actual person, make sure you have a kind tone, or approach it as a something you aim to solve! "What needs do you have? What problems need to be solved in your life?" This makes it possible to understand the audience more deeply beyond the demographics you can identify on the surface. Do not miss this opportunity to dig further into the topic and find the most relevant information in order to ensure you effectively engage and impact your audience. The presentation is, after all, not just about the topic itself or you; it is about the listeners. Without an audience, presenters would just be people talking to themselves, so why do so many people forget about the audience?

One way to consider the audience is to place yourself in the audience. For example, Ms. Kat Burks was a freshman university student who was asked to present a training presentation that offered a solution for student success. As a freshman, she was offered an unlimited meal plan to use in her college cafeteria. After months of using the cafeteria, she had experienced some lackluster meal options and saw that her fellow classmates were frustrated about options offered for meals. She chose to do a presentation called *Cafeteria Hacks* highlighting ways to make the unlimited cafeteria plan work to students' advantage. She shared ways to combine different foods to create new meals together and she shared ways to store staple ingredients like butter and cheese to take back to a dorm room. She saw the exigence, the specific need, in her own experience as she was desperate to make eating in her cafeteria more enjoyable and convenient to her lifestyle.

Audience members will seek out presenters that choose a topic that makes sense, meets their needs, and explains a topic concisely in a way that helps them understand complex ideas better. Likewise, presenters who focus on their audience's problems or needs will consistently see appreciation for their topic and find they have gained a following.

Your Passion

Passion and enthusiasm for a topic on the part of a presenter is necessary in order to achieve ease in the process of researching, writing, rehearsing, and delivering a speech. Every step of the process in creating a presentation is impacted negatively if you do not care about or have experience with the topic you choose. Passion for the topic will impact your credibility, your connection, and your confidence.

Credibility for a presenter is essential as it means you have built trust with those listening to your presentation. The presenter who is passionate about their topic will have personal stories as well as enthusiasm for the research found on the specific subject. An audience trusts a presenter who has personal experience and extensively researched their topic proving they are an authority on the topic. Without passion for the topic itself, there will be not be clear credibility on the part of the presenter.

In addition to credibility, connection is very important for a presenter as they prepare and deliver a speech. Connection can lead to credibility; however, it is much deeper than just knowledge and research. Connection is the personal reason why you are passionate about your topic. Often, it is helpful to explain the personal experiences you have with your topic whether it be that you have lived through it, or when and where and why you became passionate about it in the first place. For example, one would hope that a student delivering a speech regarding human trafficking has not personally been through the experience of being trafficked. However, they could share about the moment they became passionate about ending modern-day slavery and why they were so moved to take up the cause. While they have not lived the topic, they have passion, and the roots for that passion are where they find the connection.

Fig 12.2 You not only bore the audience but run the risk of boring yourself as a presenter if you don't have passion for the topic!

Source: https://www.shutterstock.com/image-photo/business-meeting-employees-office-1044518494

When presenters do not have passion for their content, it makes research boring and seems to drag on (Fig. 12.2). Lack of passion makes it hard to try to rehearse because the topic bores even them! And delivering something that is not special or important to you will make you less confident when you deliver the presentation itself. Confidence goes a long way to engage the audience and show them the kind of excitement, passion, and joy your topic can bring to their daily lives! The reason lack of passion negatively impacts confidence is that the low interest throughout the full speech curation process means a presenter will most likely not be as prepared because they either rush the process or do not give enough effort and thus are not as knowledgeable. Once on stage or in front of an audience, the lack of care or passion shines through in the form of reduced or no confidence on the part of the presenter.

Passion is necessary. Think about your college classes. The professors that stand out for better or worse are because of their passion or lack thereof for the topic. Think about professors of history, math, English, psychology, and much more. They should deliver lectures with excitement and clear communication to the audience about why this content is necessary or important to know! Why then, are there some professors that are boring and tired in how they deliver the subject that they have pursued to the point that they have continued education for many years after undergraduate study to teach it? Maybe they have lost passion or maybe they have not learned anything new. Whatever the reason, the lack of passion will impact the purpose and goals for the presentation as well as lose the audience.

As you can see understanding the purpose of your speech, knowing who your audience are and why they should care, as well as being passionate about a subject combine to create a well-researched, composed, and delivered message. Crafting content will be much easier to achieve if you consider these three factors and, in the end, you will be left with a strong message that can easily be dynamically delivered.

TAKE ACTION

Scenario: You have a speech regarding pet peeves to deliver to a group of college students similar to the one described in the chapter. Think about the purpose, the audience, and your own personal passions and jot down some of the things you would use such as supporting material, goals, and personal perspectives.

1. What would be a potential purpose and goal with this particular presentation?

   _____

   _____

   _____

2. Who is in the audience? If you are a college student, consider your classroom and imagine the level of diversity in the room and jot down things like demographics, ideas that may address an urgent problem or need, or even topics to avoid:

   _____

   _____

   _____

3. What are you passionate about? Most people tend to get a little heated talking about their pet peeves. So, finding passion may not be hard in this instance. But consider what you care about, what does that pet peeve say about your passions? Write down ideas regarding what topic to address and why you chose it/them:

   _____

   _____

   _____

13 | Outline Layouts and Styles

Staring at a blank screen. We have all been there. Writer's block is not just for papers, it applies to a speech outline too. What is the best outline for a speaker? Should every word be written out? Should it only be key words? Should it be phrases? The great thing about outline layouts and styles as you walk through the process of drafting your presentation is that you can adapt and change how you outline content in order to help you deliver your speech the best way possible. There is no right way. There are, however, layouts you can use as guides to create your best possible outline. Two outlines that you will learn in this chapter are the two opposite ends of the spectrum: a Roman Numeral presentation outline and a Sandwich Structure presentation outline. We will look at the elements in each outline and then also talk about best practices when crafting an outline to make speech delivery smooth. Looking at those layouts, you may just find the best option for you or be able to adapt parts of them to create the best outline that helps you confidently deliver your speech.

Roman Numeral Outline

The Roman Numeral outline is well known. Looking back on any class you have taken that requires an outline of some sort, the key example taught is the standard Roman Numeral outline format. The Roman Numeral format includes a speech title, thesis, introduction statement, main points indicated by Roman Numerals (I, II, III), subpoints indicated by letters (a, b, c), written transitions, and a conclusion statement.

Let's start at the top. You will place the speech title then below type out your thesis statement, followed by an introduction. Script this introduction to be simple, not too wordy, and clear in order to grab the audience's attention. Using techniques discussed in Chapter 8 to create an introduction that achieves best practices will help you create this introduction statement. In addition to an introduction, include the preview statement in this same section of the outline.

Directly after the introduction and in between the main points place a typed and scripted transition statement. (Building a transition can be reviewed in Chapter 9.) The transition should not be lengthy and take up minimal lines of your page.

Your main points will each be numbered with a Roman Numeral and be followed line by line with subpoints labeled with lowercase letters. You choose and craft the information shared on the main points. This can be sentences, phrases, or simple words.

After the main body of the speech, the next section will be the conclusion and should also include a review statement. (Remember to review best practices in Chapters 8 and 9 on building these elements of your speech.)

Pros and Cons of Roman Numeral Outlines

Roman Numeral outlines are excellent in that they are very organized, they isolate each element of the presentation, and with the vertical orientation of the page you have a full line for each item if you want to provide sentences or more detail for each subpoint. With that being said, the challenges this layout offers could be detrimental to the delivery if a presenter gets distracted or off track. Arranging content in a vertical layout can make it difficult for a presenter to find their place if they get sidetracked. Because everything is in a single column, you may spend a lot more time paused looking for your place if you are distracted. Another negative side effect of utilizing a Roman Numeral outline is that there is more temptation to load the outline up with every single word you want to say. Because you have a full line to include information for each subpoint, you are more likely to write more information on the page, which then leads to more reading of the outline rather than dynamically delivering the content. Reading the outline can lead to no eye contact and less engagement of the audience. Putting too much text on the outline can be very detrimental to delivery style and impacts rehearsal. When every word you plan to say is written on your outline, there is a higher probability that the amount of rehearsal will be less than normal because there is comfort knowing everything that is needed to be said is on a page in front of you. This creates a false sense of security and then when nerves pop up, presenters lose their place and struggle to get back on track.

Another difficulty with the Roman Numeral outline is that often you could utilize more than one page (as you will see in the example in Fig. 13.1). Having multiple pages can not only be distracting to the presenter but also distracting to the audience as the presenter flips through the pages of their outline. If your Roman Numeral outline goes over one page, make sure that when you present you have both pages laid flat rather than having to flip through during your presentation.

Example of Roman Numeral Outline

Fig. 13.1 is a Roman Numeral outline by Nic Noland (2021), a graduate of The University of West Alabama. Nic utilizes best practices in creating the introduction, the transitions, and building main points that all support his thesis. You'll notice that every element is comprised of summarized statements. The introduction is more detailed, and the main points and sub points are very brief descriptions of the information he wants to discuss. While this is very helpful it does not cover every word he will say in the presentation so as not to lose the opportunity to have conversational style.

TOPIC: Pancakes: the history of one of humanity's favorite foods.

THESIS: Pancakes are one of the most popular foods that exist. I want to show why that might be to show more context to one of the world's favorite foods. It also might give you some inspiration for the next time you get flippin'.

INTRODUCTION

a. **Attention Getter**
   i. In the U.S. a alone, we've call them pancakes, hot cakes, flapjacks, griddlecakes hoe cakes, Johnny cakes, and slapjacks. They've also taken the form of French crepes, Yiddish Blintz, Russian blini, Scottish bannocks, Japanese okonomiyaki, and Latin *alita dolcia*. As long as humankind has had the option, we've chosen to eat pancakes.

b. **Reason to Listen**
   i. Pancakes are almost universal to life. They can tell us a lot about ourselves, and learning how people across time have enjoyed them is how we continue to share this tradition. This will help you take your pancake game to the next level.

c. **Thesis Statement**
   i. Pancakes are one of the most popular foods that exist. I want to show why that might be, and what it can tell us about ourselves. It will also you some inspiration for recipes the next time you get flippin'

d. **Preview of Main Points**
   i. First, I will provide a brief history of pancakes.
   ii. Second, I will discuss the popularity of pancakes
   iii. Finally, I'll discuss pancake benefits

I. a. The first pancake: The romans lay claim to the invention of the first pancake-like-things, *alita dolcia*. But analysis of Otzi the Ice Man, a 5,300 year-old preserved body, show that he also enjoyed pancake like foods.
   b. Europe: All the unhealthy things in the cupboard in Europe had to be disposed of on Fat Tuesday (Also called Shrove Tuesday) right before lent. Butter, sugar, fats, and eggs all had to be used to avoid temptation the next forty days. They mixed them all together. In Australia, the UK, and Ireland, this is called "Pancake Tuesday."
   c. It didn't take long for this tradition to spread to the colonies. The United States created its own recipes for "griddlecakes" "hoe cakes" and several other names before it had even declared independence.

Fig 13.1   (*Continued*)

(Continued)

TRANSITION: Now that you know the history, let's discuss why pancakes are so loved.

 II. Raise your hand if you LOVE a good pancake. If you're not raising your hand, you're either lying or you didn't understand the question. Everyone loves pancakes and there's clear reason why.
   a. They're versatile.
       in Europe, they're made with sherry, spices, and nutmeg, fruit, or some combination. many regions have adapted wheat pancakes into savory dishes, such as the French. Region Bretagne's "galette," a crepe folded around meats and cheeses, or blintzes, which are Yiddish and either sweet or savory.
   b. They're practically a sport.
       They're fun to cook. In fact, so fun, that we've been playing games with them forever. Pancake races started in England in 1445. In 2010, one man ran a marathon at Niagra Falls while flipping a pancake once every two seconds.

TRANSITION: All across the world, we call pancakes something different, and we all make them a different way! So, why are we so obsessed with pancakes?

 III. Pancake benefits
   a. They're comfortable, identifiable, and they remind us of home.
   b. They're easy to make. The ingredients are found almost everywhere in the world
   c. So whether it's to celebrate Pancake Tuesday, win a contest, enjoy breakfast, lunch or dinner with our families, the world seems to agree that pancakes are one of the best ways to do it (especially for Pancake Tuesday).

Conclusion

   d. I've talked about pancake history, why we like them, and what makes them so important.
   e. Restate thesis
       i. Pancakes are one of the most popular foods that exist. I have shown why that is. Next time you go to make breakfast, maybe you'll try throwing in some nutmeg, honey, apples into your pancake pan, and maybe attempt a world record while you're at it.

Fig 13.1 (Contributed by Nic Noland)

Sandwich Structure Outline

The Sandwich Structure outline is a unique format created by Christine Clapp and Bjorn F. Stillion Southard. In their book *Presenting at Work: A Guide to Public Speaking in Professional Contexts* (2014), they recommend utilizing this format because of its unique

Chapter 13: Outline Layouts and Styles 85

ability to promote extemporaneous style in presentations. The Sandwich Structure outline differs from a Roman Numeral outline as it is only allowed to fill one page, it is oriented in a horizontal layout, it fully scripts the introduction and conclusion, and it has some visual elements to remind you of your presentation cues.

Let's start at the top of the outline. At the very beginning of the page, you will have a fully scripted paragraph, which will be the exact statement you want to make for your introduction. Because introductions and conclusions are the most important parts of a presentation as they are most vividly remembered, they must be scripted in order to meet the exact message created by the presenter. This ensures that even in a nervous moment you will be able to know exactly what you wanted to say. This is important because the rest of the presentation on the outline is unscripted and left more open so that way conversational style will flow more naturally.

Directly below the introduction, there is a visual element that says "preview"; this is just a reminder to include the presentation cue that we've discussed in Chapter 9, where you will state the list of your three main points.

Beneath the preview, you see from left to right your main points. Having your three main points in a horizontal column rather than a vertical column allows for easy recovery if a presenter blanks during their speech. Having your three main points isolated in the center of the horizontal page also allows you to diagnose if your main points are unbalanced. When looking at points side by side rather than on top of one another, it is much easier to identify if one main point is very heavy on information and another is very light on information.

Between each main point, you will see a letter "T" inside of a square. Clapp and Southard (2014) call these *T boxes*. This is a visual element reminding you to say your transition at that point in the outline.

Just below the body of your presentation, you will see another visual element that says "Preview" reminding you to restate your three main point titles (see Chapter 9 for more details on crafting a preview).

The very last section of your Sandwich Structure outline is going to be your conclusion statement. As is the case with the introduction, the conclusion statement is fully scripted because again the audience will remember the first and last thing they hear the most vividly.

Pros and Cons of the Sandwich Structure Outline

As with the Roman Numeral outline, there are also pros and cons when it comes to the Sandwich Structure outline. Because the Sandwich Structure outline is only on one page, you are limited to how much text can be stated within each main point. The goal here is to ensure that the speaker is conversational and not reading the entire presentation. However, it can be difficult to not have full phrases or statements for the body of your presentation if you are limited on rehearsal time. Having less text and a single page requires the speaker to rehearse more often to ensure that they know exactly how they want to present each main point and their subsequent points.

Another limitation to the Sandwich Structure outline is that presentation cues like the preview, the review, and the transitions are not written out and can easily be forgotten when it comes to presentation day. Because there is only a small visual element reminding the presenter to say those presentation cues, it can easily be overlooked and not stated when the presentation is delivered.

A key to having success while using the sandwich structure outline is to rehearse early and regularly with the crafted outline in hand. This will ensure you are prepared and you remember to include those visual cues that are not fully written out on the outline.

Sandwich Structure Outline Example

Fig. 13.2 is a Sandwich Structure Outline Example using the content from Nic Noland's (2021) Roman Numeral Outline. The creators of this outline format, Clapp and Southard (2014) offer a tool on their website www.spokenwithauthority.com that helps presenters

---

In the U.S. alone, we've called them pancakes, hot cakes, griddlecakes, hoe cakes, Johnny cakes, and slapjacks. They've also taken the form of French crepes, Yiddish Blintz, Russian blini, Scottish bannocks, Japanese okonomiyaki, and Latin alita dolcia. As long as humans have had the option, we've chosen to eat pancakes.

Today I will share with you why pancakes are one of the most popular foods of all time.

PREVIEW

[T] I. History of pancakes
    A. The first pancake
    B. Europe
    C. American Colonies

[T] II. Popularity of pancakes
    A. Everyone Loves them
    B. Versatile
    C. Practically a Sport

[T] III. Benefits of pancakes
    A. Comfort Food
    B. Easy to Make
    C. Perfect for Celebrating

REVIEW

Pancakes are one of the most popular foods that exist. I have shown why that is. Next time you go to make breakfast, no matter what you call them, maybe you'll try throwing in some nutmeg, honey, apples into your pancake pan, and maybe attempt a world record while you're at it.

Fig 13.2 (Content contributed by Nic Noland)

create a Sandwich Structure outline without having to format a document from scratch. The tool allows you to identify if your content is balanced and also helps you limit how much content you include in the page by placing character limitations. This ensures that the outline stays one page is horizontally oriented, so you can have the best possible layout and includes the visual elements that will indicate the presentation cues you need to include when delivering the speech.

Pick What Works

One way a presenter can get delayed in crafting their speech is agonizing over meeting standards for presentations that aren't necessary to follow. There is not one right way to outline a speech; there is only the right way that works for you. Whether you like to do more scripting or you like to have less on a page, find elements in these examples that you like and feel comfortable using. If you don't feel comfortable with the outline that you are using, it will translate to your delivery style and come across uncomfortable to the audience. Don't stare at a blank screen, get started on your outline and fine tune it as you go through the process of crafting content, rehearsing content, and ultimately arriving at the best possible layout for you to deliver your best presentation.

References

Clapp, Christine, and Bjorn F. Stillion Southard. *Presenting at Work: a Guide to Public Speaking in Professional Contexts.* United States: Quality Books, INC, 2014.
Noland, Nic. "Pancakes Are One of the Most Popular Foods That Exist," 2021.

14 Organizing Content

There is a moment when all the research has been done and then there is a feeling of *now what?* that creeps in. Even though we know the next step is building the outline, and we know the layout we need (see Chapter 13), sometimes there is this mental wall that keeps us from really pushing forward. It's all about organizing the content. We know what we want to talk about, however you wonder, "what comes first?" And, if you do it correctly, you will also ask "why am I putting it first?" There needs to be meaning in the way you organize the research you have collected. And then once the meaning is decided, "How much information, how many points are needed?" comes to mind. There can be a method to address this madness running wild in your head and keeping you from putting pen to paper.

What Comes First and Why?

The best way to identify what content needs to be shared first and why is to evaluate what possible speech arrangement method you can use with your research. The different methods for arranging for speech content include *chronological, topical, causal, problem solution, and spatial.* Each method is arranged based on specific characteristics of content and the overall goal for the presentation. If you know why you are arranging your points in a specific arrangement pattern, it will help provide clarity in other areas such as transitions, introductions, and conclusions.

Chronological arrangement is organized by a timeline. This can start with the past or the future. Regardless of how you start, each individual point follows or precedes the other on a timeline. If your goal is to inform the audience chronological arrangement is a common method for arranging your main points.

Topical arrangement is simply organized by topic. Each individual point is its own theme or topic related to the overall goal of the presentation. Consider the speech example from earlier, *Best Desserts at Touch of Home Bakery.* Choosing specific desserts or even categories of desserts are still topical. These independent points do not need the other main points to make sense when it comes to the overall topic of best desserts; however, together they show the variety of options at the bakery and make a more well-rounded presentation.

Causal arrangement, or more commonly known as cause and effect, is where a phenomena is described and the consequences or ripple effects from that phenomena are explained. Your first main point would be the cause and the last points would be the different outcomes, consequences, or effects that occur. For example, you may want to inform the audience about the phenomena of poor sleep habits among college students. Your main points would look something like this:

1. Explanation of current trending sleep habits among college students.

2. Discussion of the causes of poor sleep habits like overwhelming workloads, limited self-accountability, and too many distractions.

3. The effects that poor sleep is having on college students like lower attendance rates, poor grades, and impact on student retention.

As you can see, explaining the phenomena, addressing the causes, and sharing the effects or the consequences of the phenomena automatically help you structure your outline and know exactly which point comes first.

Problem solution arrangement identifies a current issue and offers possible solutions throughout the presentation. Presenters can choose to explain the problem in their introduction and utilize the three main points as potential solutions, or they can choose to utilize one main point as the description of a problem and offer solutions in the subsequent main points. Unlike cause and effect, problem solution does not have fully established "causes," "effects," or outcomes at the time of the presentation. For example, if a presenter is addressing racial discrimination as a problem in their presentation, they would thoroughly describe the issue of systemic racism and, based on their research, offer what they think would be the best solutions to the problem itself. At this time, racial discrimination is something that is not resolved and does not have an established cause or effect that can be thoroughly presented. Because of this, problem solution is a better approach to arranging content because the problem is ongoing and there are many options for solutions.

When utilizing problem solution arrangement, the audience must be considered in order to find appropriate solutions that would not only motivate the listeners but also apply to their abilities and access to resources. The overall goal of problem solution is to motivate the people in the room to take action and be part of a solution for that particular problem.

Spatial arrangement, or geographical, takes a topic and explains it on three geographical levels from largest to smallest. For example, if a speaker at a university's Title IX event presents an informative presentation about sexual assault rates among college students, they may consider utilizing a spatial approach. To understand spatial arrangement imagine an image of the earth and then the image zooms in closer to the country you live in. Then after a moment it zooms in closer to have you face your own house. This is how spatial arrangement works in a presentation. The presenter at the Title IX event would start with sexual assault rates in the United States, then they would talk about rates in the state the university is located in, and then they would address local numbers within the city itself or the university campus police data related to assault on their campus if there is any. This method of organizing content helps take a big idea and zoom in on it for the audience and show them how it literally can be in their own front yard. Arranging main points spatially helps the audience understand how big issues that they never thought would affect them actually could either now or in the future.

How Much Information Is Needed?

How many points do I need? It is important to find a balance between too much and too little information. Many presentation guides recommend two to three main points because much of the research suggests that listeners are unable to retain too many points of information. Consider using *three-factor composition* when organizing your content. Three points fit nicely with the idea of a "beginning, middle, and end" for a presentation. The three-factor composition follows a rule of 3's: 3 main points, 3 subpoints, and at least 3 sources of information. If you have three main points and subpoints in the body of a presentation, it feels more complete than a two-point presentation or a five-point presentation. It is easier to follow and often provides more clarity on a topic for the audience.

The overall goal with the amount of content needs to follow the *Goldilocks principle:* not too much, not too little, just right. It is easier to hit the *just right* level when we use three-factor composition.

Push yourself to have a reason why you choose the arrangement that you do so you can clarify that message with your different speech elements from the introduction to the transitions to the conclusion. Consider why you chose your topic and what makes the most sense for a person just learning about the topic to hear first. Do not stare at your paper or computer screen wondering "now what?" anymore.

15 | Presentation Aids

A dynamically delivered presentation does not need anything to make it shine. However, the access to technology and the various methods through which we are delivering presentations in our world today can always benefit from supplemental presentation aids. While PowerPoint will remain the reigning king of the presentation aids, there are also other vehicles for supplemental aid, as well as different software programs and online platforms that help provide an alternative in the world of slide show presentations.

Various Methods

Presentation aids can range from the most complex of technology to the simplistic paper handout. The key to choosing a method is to evaluate the setting and the audience. If your presentation is delivered in a staff meeting rather than at a conference in a ballroom, the setting and the number of audience members will affect what you choose to use to supplement your presentation.

Starting with the simplest format – a paper form of handout, notecard, or even printed out infographic can be something that is considered a "takeaway aid" that can focus on the most important elements you want them to retain from your presentation. This can be simple in black and white, you can have full color, or you could include fill in the blank sections to help them follow along. Whatever you do, make sure the details are simple to read over, text is limited, and the basic elements they need to know are shared. This is best in a small setting, with a smaller audience because of the printing and supply cost associated with creating a paper format presentation aid (Fig. 15.1).

Technology has made it much easier to create content for the audience to see during a presentation. Creating a slide show with a computer helps the audience see the main points in black and white (or even some color) and can also be used to share images or video, graphs and charts, and even quotes. The most used method is Microsoft PowerPoint. The business world most commonly runs Microsoft software so it could be considered a more reliable option when presenting somewhere unfamiliar. Another slide show software is Apple's Keynote. Both offer creative layouts and designs, and they both operate similarly. The important step to take when choosing which software is to identify what computer style and operating system are available where you will be presenting. One way to ensure a slide show will translate to any system is to save it as a PDF file. You can scroll through PDFs regardless of the operating system and you can maintain your design and layout style.

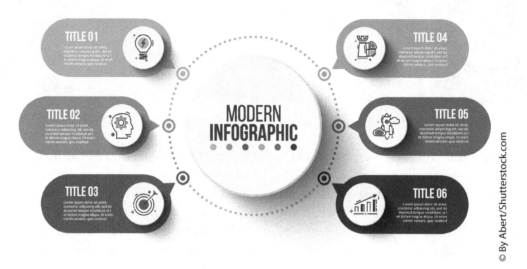

Fig 15.1 Infographics are a great way to provide hard copy take away presentation aids. They can also be used within a slide show to explain a process to an audience.

Source: https://www.shutterstock.com/image-vector/business-data-visualization-process-chart-abstract-610077995

Google Drive has become a solution for many business professionals when creating presentation aids. Google Drive offers a cloud-style storage so you can save all documents or aids. Google Slides is a slide-show-creating platform within Google Drive that can export to a PowerPoint or a PDF, or it can be opened on any internet browser and be accessed from a phone, tablet, or computer. The drawback with Google Slides is that it is limited in default font and layout options. One way to maintain your design is to import a slide show created in PowerPoint to Google Drive. Even if you have a drive with your file on it, using Google Drive as a form of backup in the event technology needs are limited will help you have confidence that your presentation aid will be accessible.

KISS – Keep It Simple... Speakers!

Many novices with presentation aids struggle with understanding format and design. Whether it is a slide show or a takeaway aid simplicity is key. The aid is a side show, not the main event. It's the background vocals to your lead. Its sole purpose is to *compliment you* not *distract from you*! So here are some areas where simplicity is key: *design, layout, and content*. Let's use slide shows as an example for these key elements.

Design

First, *design* includes the coloring, consistent elements on the slides, and the font used. Your design needs to match the tone of the presentation. Slide shows offer templates and color schemes that a presenter can choose from rather than creating their own. Not everyone can be a graphic designer, so utilizing the designed options provided is a great way to avoid the basic white slide with black text. These templates have color palates and font choices and sizes, so it makes creation easy, and design is seamless from slide to slide. The key to choosing a template is avoiding the temptation to choose something completely different from the presentation. For example, PowerPoint offers a template with little water droplets on the corners of each slide. If you presented about weather, or water safety, or even the swim team, this template would be fun and still appropriate. However, if you were discussing the sales report at work, the arts, or even current events, the water droplets do not make sense with the tone and overall topic you are presenting. Keep in mind, not every template is appropriate and not every template follows sound design principles so be very picky when choosing a template for your presentation.

Colors need to be soothing and professional. Keeping colors simple is all about choosing the right mix of colors without going overboard. Pick two to three colors to stick with for every slide. Even if you present about fun things, the colors need to match the theme you want to achieve with your topic. Darker colors for font and lighter colors for backgrounds are considered best practice when it comes to slide show design. Dark-colored text is easier to read on a light screen. Conversely, dark backgrounds are harder to read even with white text because the thin lines on many font styles are often hard to read. Err on the side of caution and choose light backgrounds – white, beige, or light grey to compliment dark text – black, dark grey, or navy. One off limits color combination that must be mentioned is red and black. While they are put together in our world for a lot of things (Hello, University of Georgia), they are never a good pair in the world of design. Red on black and black on red are not good compliments with text and backgrounds and are very hard to read. Unfortunately, many presenters still choose this because some templates offer it.

The last design feature you should keep simple is *font*. Both font style and size matter. Choosing a font that is readable from a good distance away is important to make sure your audience is able to follow your presentation by looking at the aid. Some commonly accessible fonts that are pleasing to the audience are Calibri, Times New Roman, Arial, and Helvetica. Web pages like Dafont.com, Google Fonts, and Adobe offer lots of options of more stylized fonts that have the same style or design category as these general fonts. The key is avoiding script, handwritten, or calligraphy style fonts for your full slide show. These are hard to read and often have thinner lines making them blend into the background. If you want to use something more unique and script style on the title slide, that would be the only possible exception; however, it needs to be readable. Achieve readability with more designed fonts by choosing a large font size and bolding the font if possible. When choosing font size, it needs to be large enough that someone on the back row can read it. Use a larger than normal size around 24 to 30 point font.

Layout

How many times do you sit down to a blank page or a blank slide and just stare at it? Without some established rules for how you plan to layout your slides, you could end up with too much text. In the moment, it seems easier to write out everything rather than choosing the best information to share. Keep the layout simple by getting comfortable with white space. Sometimes when crafting the slides, white space almost feels like dead air on the radio… something to avoid at all costs. With slides, that is not the case. The more space you leave around your text, the more chance that your audience will be able to see and notice the information you are sharing. When you bury important details in a paragraph of information, it is less likely the audience will see or even hear you share

© By Soikina Kateryna/Shutterstock.com

Fig 15.2 Notice the layout and design of these different slides, clean, limited content, good colors for any possible topic, and excellent font choice. Overall keep it simple!

Source: https://www.shutterstock.com/image-vector/original-presentation-templates-corporate-booklet-easy-663837895

that point of interest you want them to catch in your presentation. Consider the 4×4 Rule to make your slide layout simple: no more than four points per slide and four words per point. Now, this is not a hard and fast rule, four words per point is where this can be a little restrictive, but if your aim is to keep points to a minimum and you specifically aim for no more than four where you can, this will help ensure that your space around the slide is clean and clear of distraction.

Many speakers like to use animation features when building their layout. Animation can be distracting both to the presenter and to the audience. As a presenter, if you build animation into a presentation slide show, you must practice regularly to remember where your animation is placed. If you use animation, limit it to appear or fly in. Many animations can take seconds at a time and create awkward moments where the presenter waits for it to stop before continuing to speak. If you are new to animation and it seems complicated, it probably is. Avoid using animation if this is new to you. Avoid using animation if you are short on time. It takes extra time to build them in and keep them consistent across slides. Unless it enhances what you are talking about, choose to leave it out (Fig. 15.2).

Content

Layout goes hand in hand with the actual content you choose to share on your slides. Keeping it simple, make a slide for each main point of the body of your speech. Add in additional slides for the introduction, conclusion, and any data or visual components you want to share. On each slide, spotlight the most important information that supports your topic. For your introduction and conclusion use a photo or a quote or phrase from your speech that you are sharing at the time. For each main point slide, list out your subpoints you will be discussing. If you have data in the form of charts or graphs or you have an image or video you would like to share, give them their own slides so the audience can focus on the information and you can ensure the text is large enough to read.

One word of caution about videos is that different software and devices play videos differently. If you embed media like a video or sound file, it may not play properly at the presentation location even if it worked on your own device during rehearsal. If you have to share the media, bring a backup file or include the web link you wish to use on your slide show and have it ready to go. Arrive early and test any media you are sharing before the presentation begins and pull up your backups if the slide show does not play the media the way you planned.

10–20–30 Rule

One of the main questions students will ask when they are assigned a presentation is "How many slides do I have to have?" While the recommendations above are in order to keep things simple, it does not have to be that limited to stay simple and effective. Former Apple executive Guy Kawasaki, now a venture capitalist who listens to entrepreneurs pitch ideas, sees slide shows all the time that exceed the necessary number of slides or overstay their welcome when it comes to time spent presenting. He recommends a simple method for building an effective presentation with a presentation aid called *The 10-20-30 Rule for Slideshows* – 10 slides, 20 minutes, 30-point font. Just like the 4×4 Rule, this doesn't have to be a hard and fast rule but more like a guide to follow when you have a set amount of time to fill. Ten slides are considered the most you should have. Keep it close and you will not miss the mark on sharing the most important points in your speech content. Twenty minutes or, if you have a shorter window of time, around three quarters of the maximum timeframe you are given, should be filled when speaking. This allows time for questions if necessary and also ensures you fill the minimum timeframe you are expected to fill. Thirty-point font will be readable and easy for the audience to notice the major points you share on the slide.

Presentation aids are so helpful for the audience to connect to your speech, retain your important takeaway points, and, with visuals accompanying your speaking, they will stay engaged while you present. The key is keeping it simple! If simplicity is your aim, your presentation aid will be a winner every time.

16 | Storytelling

> "Speakers who talk about what life has taught them never fail to keep the attention of their listeners."
>
> —*Dale Carnegie*

One of the most engaging elements you can include in a presentation is a story. Also, one of the most avoided elements included in a presentation is a personal story. Why is this? Audiences love hearing interesting things about the speaker and interesting examples about the topic. However, presenters allow insecurities to cause them to shy away from sharing information about themselves. If you were to poll an audience, you would see that many of them would say they would avoid sharing a personal story on a stage. But if you ask how many of them enjoy hearing stories in a presentation, most of them would raise their hands. This is because stories engage the audience unlike any other data you can include. A story has a plot, setting, main characters, a conflict, and ultimately ends with a resolution. With such a well-rounded example, audience members can visualize themselves walking through the story or clearly understand a topic because the story demonstrates a concept that may have been foreign to them.

Many presenters avoid including stories because they are concerned that the information is too personal. If this is your mindset, ask yourself, "Have I shared this story before with others?" "Can I share this story without becoming so emotional that I am unable to speak?" "Does my story need to be shared in order to clarify the topic? Or should I use someone else's story instead?"

Have I Shared This Story Before with Others?

Many personal stories can build up emotion without us realizing it. If this is the first time you have ever shared this story, a presentation stage is *not* the place to do it. However, if this is an issue that is very important to you and you have talked with others about your personal story, then seriously consider including it in your presentation. Use a small group of people to test out your story prior to presenting in order to see how you respond when sharing in a presentation format. This will help you gauge if you are ready to share.

Can I Share This Story without Becoming so Emotional that I Am Unable to Speak?

If you know you will have emotion when sharing the story, will it be too much to where you will not be understood by the audience? Many people think they will be fine when they get on stage and ultimately, the emotion is too overwhelming, and they are unable to finish their presentation. Practicing in front of small groups of people can help you test out whether or not your emotion could get the better of you on a presentation stage. Crying or showing emotion in some way is okay! Do not discard your story because you think emotion is a turn off for the audience. Emotion can show your deep connection to the issues or topic you are sharing about, it can help the audience connect with you, and it helps the audience develop empathetic feelings toward you and your passion for the presentation.

Does My Story Need to be Shared in Order to Clarify the Topic?

First, you do not ever need to feel pressured to share your story. However, you should be encouraged that people enjoy personal stories and become more deeply connected to a presenter who is being vulnerable about their life in such a big way.

Second, everyone goes through something not only for personal growth and learning opportunities but also to *specifically to help others*. There may be someone in the audience who may be experiencing what you have gone through or could avoid hard or painful experiences by learning how you did something or hearing your personal warning about mistakes you have made. We go through things to help others, but we cannot help others if we do not share those stories that can bring light to issues, hardship, or even success!

Should I Use Someone Else's Story Instead?

Using stories does not mean you have to only utilize your personal experience. Stories or examples from history, famous people, or even friends of yours are still welcomed by the audience. It is much easier to learn the steps to take or the consequences of certain things when they are framed with a strong narrative and, ultimately, a resolution. If you feel like your story is a little too personal or you would be too emotional, don't throw out the idea of including stories altogether. Consider using someone else's story. Stories still make an impact no matter who the main characters are.

What Do I Say?

The key to storytelling is not saying too much or too little. Evaluate your story and decide what details are essential to keep the audience engaged and help them follow what you are sharing. There are always details that are not necessary for the audience to understand the story. Likewise, there are details that are necessary to maintain clarity.

There is a popular game called "Heads Up" that you can download to your phone and play with friends. In this game, your phone will give a word or phrase to your friends and they must describe it to you for you to guess the word and get a point. This exercise is an excellent way to help presenters understand what to include when sharing a story. For example, if the clue on the screen was "dog" the group could say short one-word clues like "Woof!" or "Animal." However, the player trying to guess the word may have to fill in some blanks in their mind to figure out what the group is trying to share with them. On the other hand, teammates giving clues could overshare, for example, "I have one of these at home. It is Brown, and named Rover, and they like to play catch." While the teammate guessing might figure out that it is a dog, it takes too long to follow the clues and could easily cause them to get lost in all the extraneous detail.

This example helps us understand the best practices in telling stories. Too much or too little detail can create frustration for the person trying to listen. A clue regarding the word *dog* much like a story can be simple without being too short. Clue givers could say something like, "this *is an animal* we all consider *man's best friend!*" Giving background information like settings, the characters, or props in the story, and even the conflict at hand can help the audience stay in step with the presenter as they go through a story in their presentation. Leaving out specific details or failing to set up the scenario can lead to frustration on the audience's part and maybe cause them to stop listening altogether.

The Proof Is in the Story

Stories not only connect us with the audience, but they also provide us with a level of credibility regarding the topic itself. If we have a personal connection or experience with the overall topic we are presenting, the audience are more likely to trust us as an expert in the areas we are discussing. Stories prove that we have expertise and knowledge that can be trusted by the audience. Consider a person presenting about discrimination. If a presenter has never been discriminated against, how can they really explain the experience, or even be trusted to present about this topic? Conversely, a person who has a story about discrimination can deeply connect with the audience in a way that causes them to believe the speaker and builds trust when they hear the personal experience with discrimination shared.

This does not mean you have to have personal experiences with everything you discuss. For example, if you are presenting about discrimination, a story you could include might be about the time that you talked to a friend who had been discriminated against and how it made them feel and how you felt listening. When people talk about really difficult issues like this, having a personal story is not required (and if we are good humans, we would not want them to have personal experience in that area). But the moment the presenter became passionate about that issue or the event that made them care about it more can always be a story that they include in order to encourage others to become passionate about the issue as well.

No matter the subject, Stories should always be considered as possible supporting material for presentation because it is one of the most unique ways to connect with the audience while providing examples or evidence that support their position. Ultimately, a presentation's goal should be to impact the audience and gain some type of reaction

Fig 16.1 Your story isn't for you. It's to help others. Don't let fear keep you from sharing your story.

Source: https://www.shutterstock.com/image-photo/whats-your-text-typed-on-paper-1067782139

from them. Sharing stories is one of the best ways to connect to those people listening and encourage them to take that first step toward whatever it is you are offering them with the presentation (Fig. 16.1).

TAKE ACTION

Consider sharing a story with your peers. Using the suggested prompts below, write out a story and evaluate what necessary details you should include!

- One of the most memorable experiences of my life was….
- One of the hardest days of my life was….
- I'll never forget the time….
- When I was younger, I learned….
- It was the scariest moment of my life….

Write about a story with one of the suggested starters above at the beginning:

_____

_____

_____

_____

Ethics in Presenting

"Taking something from one man and making it worse is plagiarism."

—George A. Moore

A presentation is your personal creative work, and approaching it in a way that achieves ethical best practices is necessary to maintain your credibility. If you are using someone else's words as your own, giving very little effort to craft the presentation, or presenting with ulterior motives in mind, you are guilty of unethical practices in speaking. This chapter will discuss the methods for *verbal citation, ways to promote yourself without promoting yourself, and the importance of preparation.*

Verbal Citation

In April 2020, professional motivational speaker Rachel Hollis used her platform on social media to share a quote "Still… I rise" and failed to attribute the quote to its original creator, Maya Angelou (McNeal, 2020). While she was not delivering a speech, her primary career role is motivational speaking, including her own personally branded motivation conference for women, and she used her platform to share this thought and presented it as her own work. Critics have also shared that her books and speeches have included concepts, practices, phrasing, and even titles that are nearly identical to other creative works without attribution, earning herself the label of a habitual plagiarizer. The same content from her books is what she shares in person with audiences all over the country from a podium and stage. While ethics in presenting is not solely focused on citations and credit, it is a very big part of ethical practices. It is important to have an audience that trusts you. One of the easiest ways to lose an audience's trust is to deliver content in an unethical way. Audiences must trust a presenter and if they find that they have been lied to, tricked, or the person they listened to represented work that wasn't their own, it not only causes that audience to become angry but also impacts the speaker in a way that it could ruin their career (Fig. 17.1).

How do we avoid unintentionally plagiarizing? The best way is to include verbal citations. An audience is unable to review a reference sheet while watching your presentation. Verbally sharing the creator, the source, the year, and credentialing information about the source will help the audience understand where the information came from and how valuable it is to the overall thesis. Here is an example of a verbal

Fig 17.1 Audiences love to hear motivation live and in person, but what happens when your audience finds that you are totally different on social media or use plagiarism regularly in your content?

Source: https://www.shutterstock.com/image-photo/audience-applauding-speaker-after-conference-presentation-479633347

citation in a presentation regarding mental health treatment needs among college students:

> *In his 2019 Forbes article, Garen Staglin, co-founder and chairman of One Mind at Work, shares that according to a recent study by "Penn State University's Center for Collegiate Mental Health, counseling center utilization by college students has increased by an average of 30 to 40% while enrollment has only seen a 5% increase.*

Let's evaluate:

- The Creator – Garen Stablin

- The Source – Forbes

- The year – 2019

- The Credibility – the creator co-founded an organization focused on addressing practices in mental health called One Mind at Work. Also, the data is from a research report by Penn State University's Center for Mental Health. Penn State is a well-respected university that would automatically gain credibility in the minds of the audience

- The Quote – you are sharing data shared within an article by the creator, so you have other levels of detail that not only gives clarity but boosts credibility.

As you can see, crafting a statement that still allows you to motivate or inspire without sharing the work of others as your own is important not only to show that you have done research to support your thesis but also to give your work and your character credibility in the minds of the audience.

Promote Yourself without Promoting Yourself

Using a stage or a podium to solely gain followers, get likes, and sell materials is unethical and frustrates the audience. If the purpose of the event is not specifically to sell your products, you should not use the opportunity to present to self-promote. You may be thinking, "my career requires that I get up and speak to gain customers or an audience"; this is often the case for anyone who is given the opportunity to speak. Whether you work for yourself or you work for a corporation, the opportunity to speak is an opportunity to build credibility with an audience that could ultimately become customers. However, if an event is not related to selling products, it is important to utilize your opportunity to present as a chance for people to get to know *you* better. Building trust and rapport with an audience is the best way to promote yourself without promoting yourself. When people like you for being authentic and sharing your expertise, more than likely, they will seek you out when they need the same expertise in their own daily lives (Fig. 17.2).

Importance of Preparation

Listening to a presentation is a choice. When people take time out of their day, schedule, or even choose specific presentations at a conference, they want to hear valuable information and potentially gain a new understanding of a concept. When presenters fail to put time and energy into their preparation efforts, their presentation reflects the lack of effort. Listening to half-hearted presenter deliver a speech that has very little research does not fill the allotted time, has poor delivery style, and minimal amounts of supplemental

© By Rawpixel.com/Shutterstock.com

Fig 17.2 If you are authentic in person, you will gain followers and build your brand without having to sell things from the podium. Being honest about yourself is the best way to gain loyal customers.

Source: https://www.shutterstock.com/image-photo/people-watching-video-live-streamings-1338120284

© By wavebreakmedia/Shutterstock.com

Fig 17.3 Putting in the time to prepare is the best way to ethically approach a presentation. This ensures you have accurate research and are able to deliver it in an authentic way.

Source: https://www.shutterstock.com/image-photo/side-view-beautiful-caucasian-female-executive-1464831632

material is easily considered a waste of time for audience members. Why is this unethical? The audience is one of the most valuable parts of the presentation. Approaching your presentation with only focus for yourself, whether that means you only consider your point of view, or in preparing you didn't want to spend much time, so you did very little to get it done and move on, is unethical. There is more than one person in the room and approaching a presentation in a way that it satisfies only that one person is inconsiderate (Fig. 17.3).

Be Ethical

Just remember, personal passion is only a portion of the whole picture when sitting down to craft a presentation. You still must consider the audience and the occasion you have been asked to speak at. Your whole goal should be to walk away having built rapport and credibility with the people in the room. Give credit where credit is due. Be your authentic self so people will want to support you and your endeavors. And put some time into your presentation, a creative work should reflect the best of you not your leftovers.

References

Staglin, Garen. "Addressing Mental Health Challenges on College Campuses." Forbes. Forbes Magazine, October 4, 2019. https://www.forbes.com/sites/onemind/2019/10/04/addressing-mental-health-challenges-on-college-campuses/?sh=59dd9bc0400d/

McNeal, Stephanie. "Rachel Hollis Has Apologized After Posting A Maya Angelou Quote Without Attribution." BuzzFeed News. BuzzFeed News, April 27, 2020. https://www.buzzfeednews.com/article/stephaniemcneal/rachel-hollis-apology-maya-angelou-quote.

TAKE ACTION

Using one of the following combinations, research a quote from the person, in the year, and from the source. Write out a verbal citation with the quote that you could use in a presentation:

Donald Trump 2017 New York Times	Kanye West 2009 Rolling Stone	Joe Biden 2015 Washington Post
Jessica Alba 2015 Forbes	Joanna Gaines 2019 USA Today	Marshawn Lynch 2015 ESPN

_____

_____

_____

_____

18 Preparing for Your Speech

We've all said, "I'll just wing it" and hoped for the best. Life gets in the way and things get pushed until the last minute and "winging it" is the solution we come up with. However, in the end, the results are a half-hearted, unengaging, unsatisfying presentation for the presenter and the audience! Wing it results are not the goal, but we often let time go by and put ourselves in the position to only have this option. What about breaking up the preparation into different stages so that deadlines are earlier and the quantity of work is smaller portions? Would that help? Looking at the long-, mid-, and short-term levels of preparation will help you organize the various parts of the process of preparation and make for a more engaging presentation on the day of the speech. The process of preparation is a key ingredient to success in anything you do. Founding father, Benjamin Franklin, is credited with saying, "By failing to prepare, you are preparing to fail." Let us look at some ways to prepare and see success in the end!

Stages of Preparation

Many of the stages of preparation are explained in detail in earlier chapters; however, we have not discussed where they would fall in the process of preparation. The process includes these steps: *everyday practice, assignment of presentation, choosing a topic, research, finalizing a thesis statement, identifying main points, crafting the outline, developing a presentation aid, rehearsal, rehearsal, rehearsal, following a presentation day routine, and the presentation delivery*. Some of these steps can be interchangeable based on your time availability and the presentation itself. For example, you may have a topic in mind before you are ever asked to speak. You might have researched an issue, and the assignment of a presentation prompts you to consider it as the topic. For our purposes, we will follow the stages of preparation as listed.

In the Long Term

Before you are ever assigned a presentation, you have opportunities every day to practice. *Everyday Practice* is a method of capitalizing on your daily conversations and employing accountability partners to improve your speech skills. The key here is taking advantage of opportunities to use professional sounding language and tone, identify your most

Fig 18.1 Job fairs, grocery checkout counters, daily phone conversations; these are just a few of the opportunities you can use to practice professional speaking!

Source: https://www.shutterstock.com/image-photo/career-fair-looking-highly-paid-job-1084598060

used slang and rubble words, practicing the avoidance of using rubble words that are irrelevant to the conversation, and having people you regularly chat with call out when you are using those words or slang in the conversation. Using everyday practice is helpful in getting your mind and voice unified in using proper language, tone, and pauses so that when you have an assigned presentation the practice is more natural and less forced (Fig. 18.1).

You now will be at the *Assignment of Presentation*. This is not a clever phrase; it is literally the point you are given the task of presenting from a colleague, a teacher, or a community member. When someone asks you to present, it sets off the chain reaction of the active steps toward physically crafting the presentation. When you are assigned a presentation, follow the concepts from Chapter 7 and ask the relevant questions about the occasion and the audience, and consider your interests in order to move forward in the process of preparation.

In the Mid Term

Once you know you have a presentation you will move forward into *Choosing a Topic*. Chapters 6 and 7 will help you decide the appropriate purpose to use and identify the important questions to ask yourself to guide you into choosing the right topic.

Once you have topic ideas, you will now begin the *Research*. Research can help you gauge how much or little information is available about your topic. It will show you various themes on the subject, key concepts, and individuals related to the topic.

Your research will help you identify the core idea you want to present about leading to *finalizing a thesis statement*. Narrowing down your thesis into a simple statement will help guide you in further research and future steps in preparation of your presentation. Elizabeth Segren (2019), journalist for Fast Company, interviewed many TED Talk veterans, and they recommended that the idea, or more specifically the thesis, must be "specific, digestible, and bite sized."

Using the available research, you will craft this "specific, digestible, and bite sized" (Segran, 2019) thesis statement so you can move on to building your content. *Identifying main points* and building the subsequent content are where you take the research and find the core ideas that support your thesis. Chapters 12 and 14 explain the concepts behind choosing your content, deciding what information needs to be included, and deciding how to organize the information in a clear and purposeful order.

When you determine what main points you will use and have organized the content you have gleaned from your research, you will need to begin *crafting the outline*. In Chapter 13, you see two contrasting examples that you can use to create the best outline for you to use. The key is to consider the amount of content you have loaded into your outline. Is each point being a team player and contributing the same amount of content as the others? Do you see holes in your content? Do the points make sense in that order? Even after all the research is done, there is still a chance that you need to adjust. Using the keys you learned in building an outline will guide you in evaluating if you have created a strong foundation for your presentation that will direct your efforts as you move forward in the preparation process.

Once the outline is built, you can use it to begin *developing a presentation aid*. Following the guidance in Chapter 15, you should be able to bring the content on your page to life by highlighting the key points in some form of presentation aid. Whether you are using a handout or a slideshow, visuals are an excellent way to engage the audience so they can retain the information. The key in preparation of the slide show is to create it early in the process. You must use it through the next phase of the preparation process, *rehearsal*, in order to keep the information synced with your spoken word and to incorporate it with confidence.

Now it is time for *rehearsal, rehearsal, rehearsal*. Many people fail to see this as the most important step in preparation. You have done all the work, you have researched the content, you have arranged the information, so you probably do not need to worry about running through the full speech more than a couple times right? No. *This is sarcasm.* You can *never* have enough run throughs of your presentation! In his 2013 book *Outliers: The Story of Success*, Malcolm Gladwell shares his 10,000-hour rule to achieve excellence. While you do not need to practice, nor have time to practice your presentation 10,000 total hours each time, you do learn the importance of committing time to running through the presentation. Many of the most successful TED talk speakers have dozens of hours put into rehearsal alone. It has been said that Dr. Jill Bolte Taylor rehearsed her TED talk around 200 times, or approximately 67 hours. Susan Cain has said she practiced all day for six days, or around 48 hours (Aquino, n.d.). These two women each have over 20 million views of their talks proving that rehearsal is a key element in determining how effective a presentation will be in the end (Fig. 18.2).

Fig 18.2 Rehearsal is the most important step in preparation. Take every opportunity to practice, push yourself to achieve seven full rehearsals!

Source: https://www.shutterstock.com/image-photo/mature-businessman-standing-rehearsing-before-giving-1323828806

What if you do not have six days or 67 hours to practice? Consider doing your presentation seven total times from start to finish. The number 7 is the most *prime* number, in the Bible, the number 7 is considered the number of perfection, many civilizations consider the number 7 magic, and we all know about "lucky 7" in the casino! While we know aiming for perfection is not the goal for our speech, the number of perfection, magic, or luck can refer to having a perfect amount of rehearsal that leaves the need for luck out of the equation and creates a magical presentation!

Have everything completed including your outline and presentation aid. Consider doing some basic rehearsal for the first two or three run throughs. After three times of rehearsal, you will see areas of content that need to be changed, rearranged, or updated in your delivery, or on your outline or presentation aid to improve the overall presentation. Run through four more times using your presentation aid and outline, even dress for the occasion in the outfit you plan to wear so you can get comfortable with every click, point, and word as you wear your professional attire.

Do not forget to heed the instruction in Chapter 15 about building minimal animation into slideshows. Too many clicks can create a burden on a presenter who is also trying to remember content and how to dynamically deliver the presentation.

In the Short Term

The short-term period prior to a presentation can be considered the full 24 hours prior to the presentation. The day before your presentation, you should be getting the essentials ready. How many times have you gone to the closet for the perfect outfit the day of an event to sadly find the outfit is dirty or does not fit? Then of course you stare at the dresser full of clothes or the hangers in the closet thinking, "I have nothing to wear" (Fig. 18.3). Would it be much easier to discover this disappointment earlier than an hour before you have to leave? Checking on clothes, printing out papers needed like an outline or a presentation aid, saving any files to a flash drive as well as a secondary location (such as an online cloud location like Google Drive or Dropbox), and planning your presentation day schedule *all need to be done by the evening before your presentation.* This ensures the day of the presentation does not include additional stress besides normal presentation nervousness. You probably can reflect on an important day where everything went wrong because nothing was prepared the day before. The stress that things like clothes, printers, and technology can create on the day you need them is unnecessary because you can prepare in advance. (And just remember if you plan to print anything last minute, it is safe to say the printer cannot be trusted and will always be out of ink, paper, or won't be synced, and is not worth the headache it will cause because you did not address this need the day before.) Make sure you have all the things you need the next day laid out and ready to go to avoid having to play hide and seek with your items the day of the presentation.

Fig 18.3 Don't wait until the day of the presentation to figure out your clothes, your timeline, and your food. Prepare everything a day early to make sure you don't get overwhelmed!

Source: https://www.shutterstock.com/image-photo/man-picking-jacket-closet-fashionable-wardrobe-1027205905

© By Africa Studio/Shutterstock.com

Another pre-presentation day task is to consider how long it will take you to arrive to the venue of your presentation. It is good to map out directions, maybe even drive (or walk) the route around the same time of day you will present to get a feel for potential traffic and detours as well as gain a level of comfort by knowing where you need to turn, park, and more before the day you have to arrive on time.

Now you are ready for presentation day. It is time to *follow a presentation day routine.* This is like your morning routine but with your presentation in mind. Wake up 30 minutes earlier than you need to in order to get going without being rushed and allow for any unforeseen challenges that may occur. Eat a light and energy-giving breakfast. Do not choose the biscuits, sausage, and gravy. Choose fruit, scrambled eggs, or granola, and avoid heavy or greasy foods for any meal before the presentation. The reasons you choose lighter fare for food are first to give you energy and second to fill you up without creating stomach issues. Gas or bloating should not be added to an already nervous stomach. Limit caffeine to avoid enhancing nervousness. Make sure you have a 2-hour window between your coffee and your presentation to ensure your caffeine is not accelerating any shaking nerves may create. As you get ready, run through the presentation out loud or in your head to refresh your memory and get your mind focused on your presentation. Lastly, warm up your voice, sing in the car or the shower, do tongue twisters, call a friend. Make sure that the first time you use your voice is not the presentation itself. Use your voice however you can throughout the time prior to the presentation to ensure you are sufficiently warmed up to speak!

You are now at the final stage of *presentation delivery.* All the stages you have walked through in creating the best content, notes, and presentation aid combined with the efforts in the process of rehearsal and making sure you are prepared on presentation day will allow you to have more confidence and dynamic delivery during your presentation.

Just some reminders about your presentation: arrive early, consider the common phrase "If you are on time, you are late!" Being early will give you time to survey the presentation space and get you in the right frame of mind to present. Have back up of technology and notes. Having more than one of everything is helpful in the event you lose something.

Be confident! If you have done every stage of the process of preparation you will be prepared! The more prepared you are, the less likely it is that distractions or unforeseen challenges will completely derail you when you have to present. Do not aim for perfection, aim for perfection in preparation and work to do your best. Rely on the preparation and hard work you have put in to create and deliver this presentation. Putting in the work on the front end of the presentation day will ensure a successful presentation in the end!

References

Aquino, Justin. "How Much Should You Rehearse for a Presentation?" Cool Communicator. Accessed May 8, 2021. https://coolcommunicator.com/how-much-should-you-rehearse-for-presentation-tedtalksvideos/#:~:text=There%20are%20stories%20of%20TED, least%2067%20hours%20of%20rehearsal.

Gladwell, Malcolm. *Outliers: the Story of Success.* New York, NY: Back Bay Books, 2013.

Segran, Elizabeth. "TED Talk Curators on the 4 Most Crucial Ways to Become a Better Public Speaker." Fast Company. Fast Company, July 26, 2019. https://www.fastcompany.com/90371145/ted-talk-curators-on-the-4-most-crucial-ways-to-become-a-better-public-speaker?_ga=2.227159957.926020759.1619707902-1737614169.1619707901.

19 | Informative Presentations

Informative presentations can encompass a wide variety of topics and methods, from general information, to training, to recounting history. These presentations run the risk of being very boring as they are intended to inform rather than to inspire or entertain. Delivery can be dry rather than dynamic because of the many details that are necessary to include to fully satisfy the goal of informing the audience. How does a presenter not only keep the audience engaged but also keep themselves from nodding off as they build an informative presentation? *Discussing your passion, using supporting material and visuals, building in variety, presenting a benefit to the audience, and keeping things simple* are all necessary to create an engaging informative presentation.

Discussing Your Passion

As you have learned in many of the previous chapters, your passion is the driving force behind choosing a topic, developing a thesis, and ultimately delivering a presentation dynamically with enthusiasm. It is a lot harder for a presenter to genuinely be enthusiastic about their presentation's content when they do not care about that topic themselves. Passion for a topic does not mean this content is your daily focus. However, the topic should stem from or be connected to a passion of yours. For example, maybe you are a leasing agent for an apartment community, and you have been asked to talk to new leasing agents at a company training. You are asked to talk about the job and the daily duties that are not necessarily on the job description but are part of the work. Even though you may not be passionate about leasing, it is something you do all day, it is something you are skilled at, and you enjoy helping others. These factors combine to create enthusiasm for your topic. You want to share the tips and details of how to succeed as an agent and you are encouraged that your work sees you as an expert, so this translates into the feeling of passion that stems from a daily activity that you can inform the audience about.

Using Supporting Materials and Visuals

Including facts, images, stories, narratives, examples, statistics, and more allows the information to be more digestible. Just telling an audience about something with dry information could cause them to let their mind float away because there is nothing to anchor their attention. Supporting material is a great way to keep the listener anchored to the presentation's information. Demonstrating the information in a way that translates to everyday life or shows how it applies to the listeners by using supporting material and visuals not only keeps everyone engaged but helps them recall the information they may need to know later.

Let's go back to the leasing agent example: During your informative presentation, you may include supporting material like stories about things you have experienced at work. You may include statistics about sales and commission opportunities. You may give examples of incentive programs that you have been able to participate in and growth opportunities that have been offered because of your experience in that job. Some visuals you may use to accompany the supporting material could include website information about company programs, pictures of properties that you can work at within the corporation, financial reports showing commission or sales numbers, and organizational charts that demonstrate growth opportunities.

Listening to someone talk about the day-to-day experience in a job can be very boring. However, sprinkling in these strong instances of supporting material and visuals that also matter to the audience will help engage, encourage, and maybe even inspire them to push themselves as they take on this new job opportunity. Something that could be very dry and boring can easily be turned around to be engaging and encouraging with supporting material and visuals.

Building in Variety

Informative presentations can sometimes be very data heavy. Because the presentation's goal is to fully account for the topic, sometimes presenters limit themselves to one type of supporting material like data or simple examples. The key to keeping listeners engaged is to build in variety when it comes to the supporting material you choose to use. Do not only include stories but support those stories with data, don't just recount facts or timeline information, use examples to bring those facts to life. This will ensure the audience is engaged as well as keep the presenter from being bored with their own information. The more variety you build into your presentation the more you can maintain enthusiasm in the whole process of preparation as well as the delivery! Infographics are an excellent way to share variety visually and help simplify some complicated information (Fig. 19.1).

Present a Benefit to the Audience

Audience members are only seeking out presentations to gain information that will benefit them. Even if they are required to attend an informational session, they are expecting to hear why it is important they need to know this information. That is why working to highlight the benefit to the audience early on in the presentation is important. You may have heard of WIIFM – *what's in it for me?* – this is a common mindset for anyone sitting in an audience. They want to know what this presentation has to make their lives better occupationally, emotionally, physically, personally, and much more. The key in an informative presentation is to make it very clear what the benefit you believe is for those listening (Fig. 19.2).

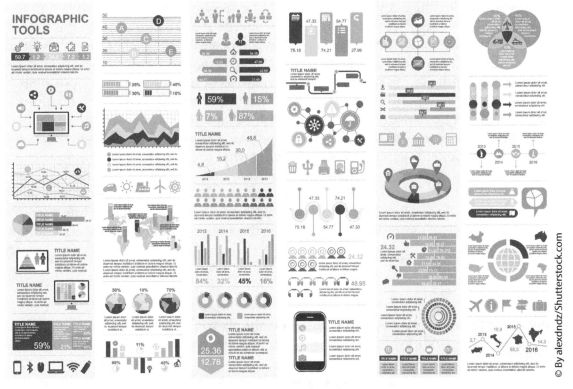

Fig 19.1 Here's an example of the variety you can build into a visual infographic. This creates a colorful engaging display of some very data focused detail without it being boring!

Source: https://www.shutterstock.com/image-vector/infographic-elements-data-visualization-vector-design-557653495

Fig 19.2 Engage the audience by providing a benefit to them. Audiences appreciate content that is focused on their needs and it is more likely that they will want to write it down to remember.

Source: https://www.shutterstock.com/image-photo/listeners-take-notes-notebookssitting-conference-room-1493006954

Let's revisit our leasing agent example one last time. If you are asked to present to new employees, they're sitting there nervous about what their daily life is now going to look like in this new job. The key is considering all of the positive things that the job brings to their daily lives. What's in it for them? Financial growth, professional development, networking, developing sales skills that can translate to other industries or positions. These benefits may be something that you have encountered working for that company. That means you can be reassuring and enthusiastic that if they work hard as an agent, they could see the same growth as you have in your personal experience.

Presenting the benefits whether it's identifying what they will learn during your presentation or how they will personally grow or benefit from the information you are sharing is one of the best ways to keep an audience engaged. If they are excited about learning those benefits on the front end of the presentation, they will absolutely keep listening to find out the secret to your success or the steps to follow to become better at a skill.

Keep Things Simple

Like Albert Einstein said, "if you can't explain it simply you don't understand it well enough." Presenting an informative presentation means you have to be somewhat of an expert on the topic. Knowing a topic thoroughly will allow you to fully explain it without it being too complicated. Keeping steps or definitions simple and matching the level of understanding in the audience will make it easier for listeners to follow what you are sharing and comprehend it more clearly. People who don't fully understand what they're talking about tend to ramble, get confused, and, in turn, confuse the listeners. Make sure if you are asked to inform an audience about any topic that it is one that you can fully understand by the time of the presentation or it is one that you have personal experience or first-hand knowledge about before accepting the request to present. The last thing you want is to stand in front of people to inform them about a topic and fail to be knowledgeable about your topic enough to speak with confidence.

Knowing your audience and staying true to your passion is the best way to engage your audience when delivering an informative presentation. Just because informative presentations can often be boring and dry does not mean they *have* to be boring and dry. Find ways to be engaging and build in variety to not only keep your audience's attention but also keep yourself engaged throughout the process of preparation and delivery. Make sure you are knowledgeable about the topic and keep things simply explained so the audience will retain the information better. Make it your goal to turn any informative speech into an engaging one and you will be a sought after speaker at any event!

20 | Training Presentations

"Tell me and I forget. Teach me and I remember. Involve me and I learn."

—Benjamin Franklin

Training is a form of informative speaking aimed at providing a learning outcome for the audience. Training is not simply intended for a school classroom. Professional organizations develop and prepare employees for daily tasks with single sessions and workshops aimed at teaching the skills they need on the job. Many people seek training to develop not only professional but personal skills. YouTube, LinkedIn Learning, Master Class, and many other websites are dedicated to teaching people skills related to hobbies, technological programs, professional development, and more. Being skilled at delivering training presentations will allow a presenter to be more flexible when asked to speak.

Training presentations must share a *learning outcome,* be *simply explained,* and offer *opportunities for active involvement* with the audience. If all of these are included, your training presentation will impact your audience and encourage information retention.

Learning Outcome

The learning outcome is a statement included in the introduction of a training presentation that tells the audience what they will learn by the conclusion of the presentation. This follows the principles of informative speaking by declaring the benefit for the audience from the outset of the presentation. Defining the learning outcome early in the process of developing your thesis will create clarity for the development of your presentation content. The learning outcome is very similar to the thesis statement. For example, if a college student is assigned a presentation with the instructions, *train the class to use a resource that promotes student success.* A student may choose to train the class to use a mobile app, Quizlet, to help improve study skills and their thesis would read: *I will train the class on how to use the mobile application Quizlet to improve their academic success.* The learning outcome would be very similar to the thesis identifying the presentation's specific goals: *Today you will know how to use Quizlet on your mobile device to improve your overall study skills.* While these sentences are similar, their roles in the preparation process are slightly different. A thesis directs the overall content; the learning outcome sets a final goal for the presenter. Both are achieved with the organization of the research, supporting material, and through the delivery.

In this example, the thesis ensures that the speaker discusses how the application Quizlet is used and in turn will identify that it is an academic learning tool. The learning outcome will direct the speaker to focus on the use of Quizlet specifically for studying and using it on a mobile device. This will lead them toward choosing proper examples of how to use Quizlet in order to study, and they may consider using research about learning styles to suggest which method in Quizlet would work for different learners.

Simply Explained

Have you ever had someone give you directions and they are not really clear about street names or only give landmarks and they fill in the details with unnecessary stories that further confuse you? (Fig. 20.1). Training without clarity and simplicity will leave your audience feeling the same. Adding in too much extra detail when teaching people how to actually follow a process could make it harder to retain the information you need them to learn. Consider the Who, What, When, Where, Why, and How as you start to determine your delivery and content. Are these questions being answered? Are you making sure you explain every step that is important to know? Are you clarifying who is eligible to do what you are talking about? Are there any restrictions or additions based on the person?

After making sure you are covering all these different questions, evaluate your supporting material. Does it achieve the thesis and the goal of the learning outcome? Do you ramble or are you only including relevant examples that will support your thesis and learning outcome? In training, the audience wants to know how something works but also want to know your personal experience. We see this with product reviews.

© By ra2 studio/Shutterstock.com

Fig 20.1 Listeners are trying to tie everything together by listening first, so make sure your explanation is simple to help them follow your presentation well and actually learn what you are training them about.

Source: https://www.shutterstock.com/image-photo/young-student-thoughtful-expression-tangled-arrows-439006402

Many people trust first-hand experience of others and a training is like a live, in person product review! A good reviewer gets to the point and shares true experiences with the product without muddying the waters by including their own personal commentary about unrelated information.

The techniques and steps you share may not be simple, but you must explain them in the simplest form in order to keep the audience engaged and help them process, understand, and retain the information you are sharing.

Opportunities for Active Involvement

Training presentations are given with the goal of achieving a learning outcome. How does a presenter know if that goal is reached? Active Involvement of the audience throughout the presentation as well as at the end is an excellent way to confirm that the information is being retained. Some common ways to involve the audience and reaffirm the main takeaways are *Think Pair Share, Quiz, and Check for Understanding*. These methods get the audience talking and help the presenter identify gaps in learning or misunderstood concepts that they will be able to correct before concluding their session (Fig. 20.2).

Active involvement can be used within each main point or after the body of the speech. *It should not be the **very last thing** you do in your presentation.* The conclusion statement should be saved for last so you have a way to naturally close the conversation or activities you are moderating.

What kind of active involvement works best? They are all effective in getting people discussing your content and reviewing what they need to know, so how do you decide what

Fig 20.2 Active Involvement like Think Pair Share can help the audience not only learn a concept but put it into practice before they go try a skill on their own.

Source: https://www.shutterstock.com/image-photo/marketing-department-team-analyzing-project-reports-1912433671

to use. The type of skill or resource you are training the audience to use will help direct you to choose the best type of active involvement. Let's look at each one and discuss how they can be used most effectively.

Think Pair Share is an activity where you provide a task or question to the audience, you pair or group people together and give them some time to create a response, and then they share with the audience when time has expired. Think Pair Share is best used when you have a more open-ended question, you are requiring creation of new content, or you are posing a problem that must be solved. Typically, Think Pair Share will require actually walking through the process they just learned and presenting their results. Think Pair Share takes longer than the other forms of active involvement and should be reserved for a presentation that has a good amount of allotted time. In a classroom setting, most students only have a few minutes to present; this active involvement would not be the best option for their training presentation. However, there are other scenarios where someone is given a full class or workshop session of time, which would provide more of an opportunity to group the audience together. For example, in the Take Action section of Chapter 17, you are asked to create a verbal citation for some different combinations of sources, dates, and publications. This would be an excellent Think Pair Share activity based on the training of that chapter's content. Grouping three to four people together to create a citation based on the steps learned in the lecture and having them share their findings with the class will allow the professor or presenter to critique their overall efforts and give feedback to help them improve.

Quiz is simply that - a quiz. Asking very specific questions that have a specific answer based on content learned in the session. Quiz can allow the presenter to see if anyone needs reminding of important steps or content based on the answers (or lack of answers) they receive. Quiz is a good way to involve the audience, not just at the end of the presentation, but even throughout the main points to keep reminding the group what they are learning along the way. Consider the student presentation we discussed earlier. If they chose to Quiz their audience about their Quizlet training, they may ask questions like, "What is the web address for Quizlet?" or "What personal information do you need to create an account with Quizlet?" "What do you call the game in Quizlet?" or "Can you find study sets already created for your topics?" Specific things that the student discussed in the presentation that they feel are important to remember can be built into Quiz questions. Quiz is short and does not have to take up much time and can be the best option for shorter training time allotments.

Check for Understanding is a more open-ended discussion fostered by the presenter. The goal for Check for Understanding is to get the audience talking and reflecting on the benefits that using this new resource or skill will bring to their daily lives. There is a lot of responsibility on the presenter to ensure the discussion actually keeps moving. "What did you learn?" is a poor choice for a question if you want to get people to actively be involved in the discussion because their subconscious answer could be "Nothing." "Does anyone have any questions?" is another poor choice because this is a closed question where the audience can just sit and stare and shake their heads "no." This is why it is important to get creative with your questions to encourage discussion! Let's go back to our Quizlet training one last time. Creative Check for Understanding questions could be

"What class would you use Quizlet for? Why?" "What is something new that you learned that you didn't know before today?" "Who has struggled to find a good study method?" "Which flashcard game or set do you want to try and why?" The key to these questions is they do not provide the opportunity for the audience to check out; it makes them consider answers that are specific to themselves and begin to apply the new skill or resource to their lives in unique ways.

"Teach me and I remember, involve me and I'll learn." Training presentations take spoken information and transform it into an opportunity to witness how to do something and try it in the moment. Developing the skill to teach and involve an audience will take a training presentation from just communicating basic information to effectively educating the audience so that they can walk away with new skills and knowledge to put into practice daily.

21 Persuasive Presentations

> **"Find out what's keeping them up nights and offer hope.
> Your theme must be an answer to their fears."**
>
> *—Gerald C Myers*

There is always a need for the skill of persuasive speaking. Have you watched as someone eloquently convinces another to give them a raise or on the less important end of the spectrum, let them have a few of their fries? No matter the stakes, persuasive speaking is a tool that can be used across all situations and can benefit those who master the skill. Being able to convince a change in attitude, actions, beliefs, or even behavior is the primary intent in using persuasion as a method for speaking. Is this just a natural talent or is this something anyone can do? In other words, is this magic or a method? It is both. Anyone can persuade, but it does take strategy and effort to create the magic of gaining audience attention and reaction. We will look at *Deliberative Rhetoric, Persuasive Appeals, Monroe's Motivated Sequence, and goals of persuasion* in order to help you create and structure your presentation's content in a way that will spark change.

Deliberative Rhetoric

The use of persuasion, or *Deliberative Rhetoric,* is a skill that can be learned and implemented whether in planned public speaking or in impromptu interactions. We often think of persuasion in examples such as a used car salesperson or the people overexaggerating their excitement on an infomercial about an electric rotisserie with unnatural and forced delivery. The fear of becoming like one of these types of presenters can cause many speakers to lean toward merely delivering informative presentations and missing opportunities to promote change. Salesmanship is persuasion; it is the dynamic delivery that can change how we are perceived as we persuade. Deliberative Rhetoric is focused on the future and the change that can be seen in that future based on response from listeners. Deliberative Rhetoric can be seen in presentations by politicians and activists. These people work to persuade a law to be passed or discuss the future of society in order to get people to hear and ultimately respond to their pleas for support.

Persuasive Appeals

Aristotle's Principles of Rhetoric (1816) includes three persuasive appeals: Ethos, Logos, and Pathos. Each focuses on an element that raises the persuasion quotient for a presentation and can be used singularly or combined to build attention and reaction with the goal to achieve change. No audience can be forced to take action in response to persuasion, but the ideas and concepts you share can plant the seed for considering action in their minds. For example, a doctor who is an expert in their field can recommend medication and treatment, but they cannot force that patient to take action. However, if symptoms increase, the patient will remember the advice and recommendations they received and may be more willing to follow that plan of treatment. Persuasive appeals serve to support those recommended steps of action or change and help an audience be closer to action by providing strong support to the concepts you will share in your persuasive presentation (Fig. 21.1).

Using *Ethos* as a persuasive appeal is focused on building your credibility. Noting your expertise, experience, or wisdom on a topic will help the audience feel like you are trustworthy and knowledgeable. If a presenter has experienced or has become an expert in what they are trying to persuade the audience to do, then the audience will feel like what the presenter recommends is a safe choice. They will listen with more confidence in the information based on the credibility.

When Steve Jobs, CEO of Apple, was asked to present the commencement speech at Stanford University in 2005, he was able to demonstrate Ethos by sharing personal stories that showed his credibility when it comes to understanding the elements in life that lead to success. He begins by sharing that his speech was the closest he had been to a college graduation, showing humility and building his presentation thesis on his perspective about success based on a degree. In his speech he shares that in the months where he was

Fig 21.1 Aristotle's Rhetoric is the basis for much of the concepts we use today in persuasive presentations. Most notable are his appeals of persuasion: Ethos, Logos, Pathos.

Source: https://www.shutterstock.com/image-photo/statue-aristotle-great-greek-philosopher-421724455

starting to wane in his interest of staying in college, he felt freer to choose classes based on things that interested him and he chose a calligraphy class. He shares, "much of what I stumbled into by following my curiosity and intuition turned out to be priceless later on." He goes on to share how the calligraphy class actually was a choice that changed the world. "I learned about serif and sans serif typefaces, about varying the amount of space between different letter combinations, about what makes great typography great." This statement shows his credibility as it speaks to his knowledge base for the next part of the story,

> "*10 years later, when we were designing the first Macintosh computer, it all came back to me. And we designed it all into the Mac. It was the first computer with beautiful typography. If I had never dropped in on that single course in college, the Mac would have never had multiple typefaces or proportionally spaced fonts. And since Windows just copied the Mac, it's likely that no personal computer would have them. If I had never dropped out, I would have never dropped in on this calligraphy class, and personal computers might not have the wonderful typography that they do. Of course, it was impossible to connect the dots looking forward when I was in college. But it was very, very clear looking backward 10 years later.*"

In this story's conclusion, Jobs is able to confirm his credibility and expertise all while showing what it meant for the future of the world of computers. This demonstrated his success and pointed to his Ethos, or credibility, when it comes to seeing how small choices lead to success, which follows the theme of his presentation.

Using *Logos* as a persuasive appeal requires presenting logic and reason within your presentation. You can do so by including various types of supporting material. Facts, statistics, examples, stories, and more evidentiary support for your position help the action you want people to take make sense. History is an excellent way to frame and predict future outcomes in a persuasive speech. Using supporting material that explains outcomes as the result of actions in the past can help an audience understand how their response to your presentation can impact their world. Alabama radio personalities Rick and Bubba often say on their program, The Rick & Bubba Show, "common sense is a superpower." And they are correct. Many audience members may not be able to automatically connect the dots without you doing it for them. You state the commonsense concepts by building the evidentiary support, *Logos*, into your efforts to persuade them.

In the 1800s, Susan B. Anthony helped found the National Women's Suffrage Association, which worked to advocated for women's right to vote. In 1872, she voted in the national election and was arrested and indicted for voting as it was illegal. After being released, she delivered a speech on her stance that women should be given the right to vote and built very strong arguments for women's right to vote using the appeal of Logos. She begins her speech by sharing how she would build her case, "It shall be my work this evening to prove to you that in thus voting, I not only committed no crime, but instead, simply exercised my citizen's rights, guaranteed to me and all United States citizens by the National Constitution, beyond the power of any state to deny." Grabbing the attention of the audience by immediately promising that by using the very words of the U.S. Constitution, she creates an expectation of evidentiary support for her position, or Logos. She continues by directly quoting the constitution, "It was we, the people; not we, the white male citizens; nor yet we, the male citizens; but we, the whole people, who formed the Union. And we formed it, not to give the blessings of liberty, but to secure them; not to the half of ourselves and the half of our posterity, but to the whole people - women as well as men. And it is a downright mockery to talk to women of their enjoyment of the blessings of liberty while they are denied the use of the only means of securing them provided by this democratic-republican government - the ballot."

She later utilizes multiple definitions to support her position that people are not simply male citizens, "Webster, Worcester, and Bouvier all define a citizen to be a person in the United States, entitled to vote and hold office." Once she has established definitions of the key word in the Constitution that she has built her argument around, she then uses that evidentiary supporting material to create a final appeal for common sense, "The only question left to be settled now is: Are women persons? And I hardly believe any of our opponents will have the hardihood to say they are not. Being persons, then, women are citizens; and no state has a right to make any law, or to enforce any old law, that shall abridge their privileges or immunities. Hence, every discrimination against women in the constitutions and laws of the several states is today null and void, precisely as is everyone against Negroes."

The strong Logos Susan B. Anthony implements in her presentation is built around evidence, definitions, specific legal documents, and she ties it up nicely with common sense – if, by definition, a citizen is simply a person, then why would laws be specific to gender or even race? Posing the details in this manner is simply magical yet still follows a method of building in a persuasive appeal so the audience is viewing the argument as reasonable, it makes sense, and is supported with facts or evidence.

Pathos is a persuasive appeal based on emotion. It uses the feelings and passions of the audience in order to evoke emotion, either good or bad, in order to inspire change in one direction or other. Pathos can gain explosive reactions as individuals could have a more intense response to emotions that are stirred within themselves as opposed to the appeals of ethos (credibility) and logos (logic, reason, evidentiary). Social justice issues, for instance, can be a topic for a presentation and with Logos it can be very easy to understand but when Pathos is involved in the appeal the audience gains more passion and empathy for the issue because they feel personally affected by the appeal you share.

Pathos is often used by activists, sales professionals, and in advertising campaigns. Evoking emotion by promising better skin or hair might be a way a cosmetic company tries to persuade you to buy their product. For example, Dr. Martin Luther King, Jr. worked to appeal to emotions of his listeners during his "I have a dream" speech. He begins to stir the audience's emotions near the end of his speech as he says, "So even though we face the difficulties of today and tomorrow, I still have a dream. It is a dream deeply rooted in the American dream. I have a dream that one day this nation will rise up and live out the true meaning of its creed: We hold these truths to be self-evident, that all men are created equal." All American listeners, regardless of ethnicity or race today, could easily identify the freedom, pride, and hope that comes from being able to say they have experienced the American Dream. He also uses pathos to focus on the ideals of family and the emotions that children can bring to parents, "I have a dream that my four little children will one day live in a nation where they will not be judged by the color of their skin but by the content of their character." Every parent would want the same for their children and by including statements that every possible audience member of any perspective could identify with; he was appealing to emotion with the ultimate goal of persuading an empathy for people of color and ultimately for equal rights from the audience.

Because of the significant comparison trap on social media platforms, many young people have a deep emotional desire to have the best photo in the most luxurious location to gain likes. This emotion can unfortunately be manipulated by building in pathos to a message. In an effort to sell tickets to his Fyre Festival in 2017, CEO of Fyre Media Billy McFarland promoted a luxury event complete with the idea that an attendee would be living like a celebrity from the moment they arrived. The marketing for Fyre Festival utilized social media influencers, supermodels, and celebrities. They were all coordinated to share a single orange square on the same day on social media in order to pique interest and stir up the fear of missing out (FOMO) within their audience. The point of view in the marketing allowed viewers to believe they would experience luxury, elitism, and be associated with celebrities. Unfortunately, this is an example where Pathos evokes good but leads to bad. Fyre Festival was a fraudulent experience for all attendees. The advertising was the only luxurious thing about the event, and the poor planning left 8,000 ticket holders stranded in the Bahamas with a sandwich dinner and sleeping accommodations in FEMA tents as a major thunderstorm rolled in (BBC, 2021). This was an abuse of the power of influence the marketers possessed and ultimately created a multimillion-dollar lawsuit for the fraud the audience experienced.

When using any of Aristotle's three persuasive appeals it is important to know the answers to the questions in Chapter 12, Choosing Content, in order to craft the best persuasive appeal. Who you are speaking to, the event purpose and goals, and the personal passion you have for your topic will help you identify if you need to include appeals of Ethos, Logos, or Pathos, or even combine some together to make your strongest case.

Monroe's Motivated Sequence

In his book, *Monroe's Principles of Speech* (1958), Alan Monroe works through a five-step process for crafting the most impactful speech possible. This sequence has since been considered an excellent method for crafting a persuasive presentation. The five steps are *Gain Attention, Establish the Need, Satisfy the Need, Visualization,* and *Actualization.*

Step 1: Gain Attention – This is already a step in building an introduction. Gaining the attention of the audience will get them listening to you. For example, if you wanted to discuss the effectiveness of your stain remover product, you may pose a question or tell a story about a terrible stain that most people might experience. Grass, pet, or wine stains are common in households and are often used as examples for detergent or stain remover commercials. You may ask a question about if they've ever spilled something and thought they were stuck living with their carpet looking like a Jackson Pollock painting. Maybe you tell a story about the time that you spilled wine and thought you would never be able to wear that shirt again. These examples are common things that happen to everyone in everyday life and being able to share similar perspective about that problem will help get them ready to listen to what you have to say next. Using attention getting devices tailored to the topic you wish to persuade your audience about will start your presentation off strong.

Step 2: Establish the Need – After you've gained the audience's attention, you need to convince them there is a need or a problem in their lives. Once you've shared your experience to gain their attention, turn the focus on the needs of the people in the room. Remind them that they have also experienced frustrating or disappointing moments where a stain seemed like it was hopeless to remove. Let them know what they need. Share with them that there is a stain-removing solution out there that could solve this problem that they are experiencing.

Step 3: Satisfy the Need – Once the audience understands that they have a need that must be satisfied, you can share with them your personal solution. The key is not just to tell people that you have a product that removes stains, but to demonstrate utilizing visuals or statistics and facts that your solutions satisfy their need. In the example of a stain-removing company trying to present their product to audience members, you would probably show the actual stain remover removing a stain from an item of clothing or carpet. You may also show survey results from customers or reviews that have shown real-life experiences to persuade them that you are not the only person who believes this product works. Building strong evidence that your solution works the best will help you build a sense of satisfaction for the audience.

Step 4: Visualization – It is important to paint a verbal picture for the audience so that they can Visualize what their life is like with or without your solution. You can help the audience with visualization by creating *a positive factor, a negative factor, and a contrast factor.* A *positive factor* is a statement that helps them see what the situation would look like if they utilized your solution that you provided. For example, in the case of your stain remover you are trying to sell, you can help the audience understand that they will never have to worry about permanent stains again if they use your product. *A negative factor* would be describing what their life would look like if they never used your solution or gave it a chance. While trying to persuade people to purchase a stain remover, you can remind them that their life will still be stained if they do not use your product. With *the contrast factor*, you would present both positive and negative factors. First, you would share the negative factor and then the positive. This way, the audience will be able to see what life would be like without the solution and then be provided with a positive perspective if they were to accept your ideas.

Step 5: Actualization – Actualization or the encouragement to take action is the final step in a persuasive presentation using Monroe's Motivated Sequence. The audience must understand what steps they need to take in order to adopt your solution and feel like they are easy to achieve. In the case of your stain remover presentation, you would talk them through where they can purchase the product or provide a web address. You should also consider sharing the steps specific to your audience on how to use the product during the presentation. The overall goal of this step is to encourage the audience to respond in some way.

If you struggle feeling confident in your persuasive skills, Monroe's Motivated Sequence is an excellent blueprint for a method to follow when building a persuasive presentation. Every step should be included whether it is a main point or part of your main points. If you are including each step, you can be confident that you have built a presentation that appeals to the audience and provides arguments for your concepts and prompts the audience to take action (Fig. 21.2).

Goals of Persuasive Speaking

A common misunderstanding about persuasive presentations is that the only goal is to convert people from their current way of thinking. While this is a possible goal of persuasive speaking, it is not the only goal that you could be working to achieve. *Encouraging action, strengthening the bond, and weakening the bond* are three specific types of goals that persuasive presentations are working to achieve.

Encouraging Action is exactly that, asking the audience to do a specific thing based on your recommendations. Encouraging action is often the goal of any marketing or sales-based presentation. You tell people about a product and how to use it, and then you challenge them to purchase that product and put it to use. In order to encourage action, you may want to strengthen or weaken the bond that your audience has with your specific topic.

Strengthening the bond occurs when a presenter is trying to reinforce the perspective the audience already has. For example, political rallies are typically attended by people who agree with the political views of the politicians who are presenting. There will not be an effort to fully convert everyone in this audience. The effort is to persuade them to not only continue to support those political views but also support the politician. This can provide the audience a stronger background in the knowledge of the topic discussed so they are more connected to it and have a stronger bond with the information and ultimately the politician presenting.

Weakening the bond occurs when you discuss information about a product or a concept that

Fig 21.2 Use this as a guide to walk through the steps of Monroe's Motivated Sequence. If you cover these steps, you should be able to persuade your audience in some way to take action!

Source: Amanda Gilliland

is an alternative to what the audience may already using or thinking. For example, you may be discussing a medical issue with your audience and working to persuade them to use a medication that you sell. Typically, the audience members attending a presentation like this are already experiencing that medical issue and probably taking medication for that issue. While you may not convert the entire audience over to your brand of medication, you may have weakened their willingness to only stick with the medication they currently take. This goal is to show the audience that there are other options whether it is in a product or a concept that you are discussing in hopes that the audience starts to think differently in some way about the presentation topic.

So, is it magic? Yes. Is it methodical? Yes. Persuasion is achieved by following methods that consider your audience, your situation, and your personal passions while providing the strongest appeal for your position. Making sure that your position is fully supported whether you utilize Aristotle's rhetoric with persuasive appeals or Monroe's Motivated Sequence, if you are able to achieve the goal you set out with your topic, and provide the best supporting material for your position, you might experience a little bit of magic when you present your persuasive presentation.

References

Anthony, Susan B. "On Women's Right to Vote." November 1872.

Burgess, Rick, and Bill Bussey. Rick & Bubba Show. Accessed May 25, 2021. https://www.rickandbubba.com/.

"Fyre Festival: Ticket-Holders to Receive Money from $2m Class Action Settlement." BBC News. BBC, April 16, 2021. https://www.bbc.com/news/world-us-canada-56777716.

Jobs, Steve. "2005 Stanford University Commencement Speech." June 14, 2005.

Monroe, Alan H. *Monroe's Principles of Speech*. Chicago, Ill. u.a.: Scott, Foresman and Co, 1958.

TAKE ACTION

Scenario: you are asked to deliver a persuasive presentation to convince potential college students on a summer college tour to attend your favorite university. Fill in the following prompts to consider your persuasive goals and craft the best presentation content using Monroe's Motivated Sequence and Aristotle's persuasive appeals.

1. What is your goal? To weaken or strengthen the audience's bond?

    _____

    _____

2. Use Monroe's Motivated Sequence to persuade these students to attend your school. Write a short sentence summarizing what you would include to achieve each step:

    *   Gain Attention: _____

        _____

    *   Establish the Need: _____

        _____

    *   Satisfy the Need: _____

        _____

    *   Visualization: _____

        _____

    *   Actualization: _____

        _____

3. Consider using Aristotle's Persuasive Appeals. What would you consider saying when using Pathos, Logos, or Ethos?

- Pathos appeal: _____

  _____

- Logos appeal: _____

  _____

- Ethos appeal: _____

  _____

22 | Impromptu Speaking

> **"Always be yourself and have faith in yourself.**
> **Do not go out and look for a successful personality and try to duplicate it."**
>
> —*Bruce Lee*

Impromptu Speaking is, just that, impromptu. No clear topic, no real subject until you are in the moment. It is off the top of your head, on the spot speaking. Opportunities for impromptu speaking come in the form of interviews of any kind, meetings, conversations, or question and answer sessions. The foundation of impromptu speaking is found within the speaker. The core research for your speech is based on your current knowledge, experience, or perspective. If the topic is outside of your existing understanding, it is not a speech you have to give. In this chapter you will learn *how to prepare when you are not able to prepare, build responses using a personal focus, and having a response when you do not have one.* Impromptu speaking is not a method you will use often; however, it will be a method that you will need to be able to master for daily professional activities.

Preparing When You Are Not Able to Prepare

You may be wondering, "how does someone prepare for an on-the-spot presentation?" The answer is simple, do not prepare for a speech, prepare for opportunities to speak. Look ahead. Do you have a job interview? Do you have a meeting? Do you have a training that may require questions to be answered? Are you planning a big event? Do you have a press interview? Will you be in a class or meeting expected to participate? If you know what situations will be coming your way, you can consider what questions or opportunities may arise and have a few statements on relevant topics prepared for the occasion. Your hobbies, profession, current project or event, or your expertise could all lead to moments that call for impromptu speaking.

Consider a job interview. You would not just dress up, print a resume, and head over to meet with an interviewer. You would need to consider what kind of questions an interviewer would ask: What are your strengths and weaknesses? Why are you a good fit for this job? What interests you most about this company? Once you evaluate the potential questions, then you would need to know the responses you could have including some details that build credibility behind those responses. You can research the company and form an opinion or identify things you like about them, you can have key strengths and stories about using those strengths in other jobs or activities, you can consider weaknesses and how you are trying to improve them, and you can know the job description and identify where it perfectly aligns with your experience and passions. Anticipating common topics and questions that will arise related to whatever activity you have coming up will help you with impromptu speaking.

Making sure you have data, experience or stories to share will ensure you sound credible in your impromptu speech. If it sounds on the spot without clear evidence to support your response, it will look like you are just badly winging it and overall uneducated about the topic. If you have data, details, and a personal story behind your opinion, you will sound fully confident and educated and will be received as an expert.

Make It Personal

Knowing what kind of encounter you will have will help you look deep within yourself and identify a perspective (and why you have that perspective), an example or story you could share, or personal knowledge you may want to reference in the moment. Remember, this does not just apply to interviews. Hobbies, a current project or event, or even professional expertise could all lead to moments that require impromptu responses.

For example, if a college student in a leadership role with a service organization was having a fundraising event, they should review the event's purpose, the goals for the event, who will benefit from the funds raised, know why they have chosen to be involved in the organization, and be knowledgeable about the organization as well. Now, they may not have all of that perfectly formed into stock responses, but when the event is coming up and they know there is a potential for a press interview, they can prepare responses in advance using their personal experience, knowledge, and perspective.

Athletes are often put into impromptu scenarios with press conferences and interviews as well. Many NCAA Division 1 college programs work with athletes on communication and impromptu speaking to ensure verbiage used is consistent, topics that are off limits are avoided, and overall tone is appropriate. Athletes on a football team, for example, will need to have a professional opinion of their teammates and coaches, they will need to know their opponent, they should know the proper names and roles of administrators, they should be using the proper name of the institution and team they represent, and they should understand where they are ranked or what the game that week means for their championship chances. All of these subjects are things they can have perspective about or can educate themselves about very quickly.

Personal perspective is different from opinion. Often, in professional settings, an opinion may not be the best response as it could not align with the organization you represent. Be sure to have the best professional perspective prepared for outsiders who may ask for input or ask questions of you. Consider the athlete example, maybe they do not like working with their position coach, or they disagree with the amount of playing time they are receiving. If asked about the coach or playing time, they should still respond positively and honestly. They may not say, "I really like Coach G," as this would be dishonest, but they can say something that is honest like, "Coach G. is very experienced and knows how to develop a good game plan." While they may not love the game plan or like the coach, these are true statements that will still reflect positively on the team they represent and in turn show that this athlete is a team player and above mudslinging and complaining.

Personal perspective and knowledge are the only base of research you have at your disposal when placed in impromptu speaking situations. Pairing this with preparation for impromptu speaking opportunities will help the speaker be ready in the moment, or on the spot.

Having an Answer When You Do Not Have an Answer

Impromptu speaking often is a professionally curated response to questions in all types of scenarios. Sometimes, there is no knowledge, experience, or perspective that can be used to respond because you may not have an answer for that particular question. You must still have a response to this situation prepared so you still look and sound professional in the moment. Consider the event and the best way to respond when you cannot respond. For a question and answer session after a training, you may be asked about a topic or task related to your presentation but it is outside the scope of your work on the topic. What could you say if you did not have an answer? What if you are an athlete or an organization representative who is asked about a recent current event you have not heard about yet? What if it is a topic you do not really want to discuss?

The goal is to be honest. You may be limited on knowledge and experience, which impacts your perspective significantly. Consider using responses like, "I have not researched that information, but I would be happy to look into it and update you. Let's exchange information later." Or "I honestly have not heard or read about that today, so I will have to look into it before I can share my perspective." Or "I appreciate you wanting to know that information, but I'm not able to comment on it at this time."

Honestly is the common theme across all of these tips for impromptu speaking. Make your goal to be honest and professional when you interact on the spot with people. Practice the responses you want to remember to say if asked. Research to build up your knowledge and accurately represent the people and places and things you are speaking for. Reflect on your personal experiences to show your credibility. As suggested by Bruce Lee, "be yourself."

TAKE ACTION

Gather a group of friends or fellow students together and assign each one a topic prompt from the following list. Give everyone 2 minutes to collect thoughts and run through their response. Each person must deliver his/her impromptu speech in under 60 seconds. If the response is not complete when the 60-second timer goes off, the speaker must wrap up with a closing sentence. If the person fully responds in under 60 seconds with a conclusion that's ok too! Have fun! Consider using humor or research! Be honest and include your own personal perspective!

TOPIC PROMPTS

- WHAT IS THE BEST WAY TO EAT AN OREO?

- IS THE GLASS HALF FULL OR HALF EMPTY? AND WHY?

- BAD BREATH

- TELL US YOUR BIGGEST FEAR

- WHAT MOVIE WOULD YOU WATCH OVER AND OVER AND WHY?

- CITY OR COUNTRY LIVING? WHICH IS BEST?

- DESCRIBE THE PERFECT DATE

- WHAT IS YOUR FAVORITE THING ABOUT YOUR JOB/SCHOOL?

- WHAT IS THE BEST ATHLETIC TEAM?

- WINTER OR SUMMER OLYMPICS AND WHY?

- WHAT IS YOUR PET PEEVE?

- WHAT HOLIDAY WOULD YOU SAY IS THE BEST HOLIDAY IN AMERICA?

- IS DAYLIGHT SAVINGS TIME NECESSARY?

23 | Interviews

"Be yourself."

—Genie to Aladdin

Many of us would agree that job interviews can be uncomfortable. It is hard to find the right balance of humility and confidence. Finding the middle ground between the two is narrow and tends to lead to some various personalities and behaviors that typically will not be appreciated by the interviewer. There is the unprepared person, the person who feels embarrassed about talking positively of themselves so they are too general, and the person who is overly confident and comes across arrogant causing them to take over the meeting. How does a person find the balance? *Understanding the purpose of an interview, preparing for the interview, building credibility, and being genuine* will help you form the right mindset to be ready for an interview and have confidence.

Understanding the Purpose of an Interview

Interviews are an opportunity to get to know potential candidates to verify if they are a strong fit for their culture. What does culture mean in this context? This simply is the tone of the workplace and the personality of the employees and the business. Everyone can reflect on other jobs and remember when they just felt like a bad fit with the people, were left out, and did not have passion for the work they were hired to execute. Those jobs that hire people who are not a strong fit for the culture create a miserable experience for new and existing employees.

This being said, the goal of an interview is to get to know the candidate personally beyond what is listed on their resume. Knowledge and expertise are found on a resume. A resume is required to apply in most settings. If you have been selected for an interview, this means that *you are already considered qualified* to do the job well. All that is left is to evaluate if you will complement the culture with your personality and passions.

Hear this: you have been deemed CAPABLE of doing that job well by receiving an interview. Do not walk into an interview with the questions in your mind, "I wonder if I can do this job…" or "I hope they think I am knowledgeable enough…" Why? Because YOU ARE. Your resume shows your level of expertise and receiving an interview should make you confident that YOU CAN do the job. Now all that is left is to be authentic and honest about yourself in person so they know if you fill the needs of the culture in their business.

This is the purpose of interviews. The hard work of applying has been done; all that is left is being your best self.

Preparing for the Interview

First, you need to prepare the content for your interview responses. This seems impossible; we do not know the questions, right? Wrong. Refer to Chapter 22, Impromptu Speaking, to remind yourself that any impromptu situation can be prepared for by using your personal knowledge and experiences. The difference in content for an interview versus another impromptu scenario is that it must be relevant professional content that can be applied with context to any question that may be used in an interview. How do you craft a response that can go with almost any question? Consider your personal strengths and then share a story about your experience seeing that strength used positively.

Make a list of every possible strength you have. Do any words stand out? Are there synonyms for those words that are more creative and unique? Some common general strengths people may use in an interview can include words like organized, hardworking, a leader, and more. The key to narrowing these down to more clear and creative words is to ask yourself, "In what ways am I _____?"

For example, how are you organized? Do you have a system for everything? Or do you have things clean and tidy? The synonyms for organized are more specific. So, if you like labels, systems, or formulas in your methods for organization, you may want to say that you are *formulated* rather than just organized. What about hardworking? How are you hardworking? Do you take initiative? Are you a finisher who sticks with the project and keeps it a priority until it is done? Are you able to take on surprise challenges and not let them deter you from doing the job right? Another word for hardworking in this case could be *initiator, self-starter,* or *dedicated.* The key is to make sure the word clarifies exactly what you mean.

Building Credibility

As you build your strengths, consider developing around three to four strengths with more detail by crafting a story from your personal experiences. Sometimes, the best information you can share in the interview is an experience that is not shared on the resume, but it still shows how you demonstrated your strength in a more personal way. Sharing the story can give the interviewer a glimpse into your personality, your hobbies, your background, and more of an idea of how you would fit with the culture in their business. Look at activities like sports, arts, STEM, clubs, and organizations that you have spent time with to cultivate a story about your strength. Consider experiences like travel, moving, or even life transitions like graduating or becoming a parent as settings for your stories you share.

Stories not only show your personality but also offer some evidence that you actually are what you say you are. If you are organized, a story gives the proof that you are organized. It shows how you are organized and it can even give them insight into other skills you may have. Using these stories allows you to be honest about your strengths with proof so that you do not feel like you are bragging. Sometimes it can feel uncomfortable talking positively about ourselves so a story helps us alleviate the fear that the interviewer will think we are just boasting rather than being honest.

Being Genuine

Sharing these stories can also make your interview more memorable to the interviewer. You may have a story or experience in common that make you stand out. Often companies interview 10 or more candidates on the first round of interviews. Standing out is important to make it to the next level. The key to standing out is by being professionally open, honest, and vulnerable rather than just saying things you assume an interviewer would want to hear. This will show you are being as authentic as you can for them and help the interviewer get a good sense of who you are and how you interact with others.

If you are open and honest about who you are and show your true personality in an interview and still are not hired, stay positive! They did you a favor by not choosing you. (Are your eyebrows lifting in skepticism?) If you are hired by saying and doing all the right things but they are not a true representation of yourself, then you will be right back at the example in the beginning of this chapter – miserable, left out, passionless about your work and dying to work somewhere else. If you do not get a job, it means you were not a good fit with the culture (think of them saying, "it's us, not you.") and you should be glad you still have the chance to pursue a possible perfect fit opportunity. If not, you are taken through the process of learning a new job only to discover months of time had been wasted in a job that you were not supposed to have in the first place.

Take a look at the image in Fig. 23.1. What is in the jar? Jam, gravy, preserves, syrup? Once you narrow that down, what about the flavor? Let's say it is jam. The dark red color could mean strawberry, raspberry, cranberry, cherry. What if it is sun-dried tomatoes that look like jam? Why can we not 100% say what is in the jar? Because the label is *blank*. Until the person who makes that jam puts a final label on the jar, we spend our time guessing, or worse, put our own label on the jar and make it a very unpleasant experience for the person who takes a bite. If they choose the jar because they think it is strawberry jam only to get pureed sun-dried tomatoes, they will be unpleasantly surprised and ultimately disappointed.

The same goes for an interview. If you tell a story without sharing your strength explicitly in the beginning, then you leave it up to the listener to determine what your strength actually is. Do not leave it up to anyone else to create a label for you. State your strength early and often in your story, so they know up front what your label is. For example, you might tell a story about a time you were on a team, and you had to overcome some challenges with that team. Unless you explicitly state your strength of being an initiator, the interviewer may want to give you the label of leader or collaborative or organized based on the details in your story. But what if those really are not strengths of yours? Then when you

© By bogdan ionescu/Shutterstock.com

Fig 23.1 What's in the jar? Do you know?

Source: https://www.shutterstock.com/image-photo/jar-label-70419019

are hired and they expect strong organizational skills, they will be sorely disappointed because you did not clarify exactly what strength you wanted them to know about you which was that you were an initiator. What they think you will bring to the team is actually different from who you are and that can potentially be a disappointing scenario for you both.

When preparing for an interview, build these narratives about yourself making the strength the main character and practice them regularly. Consider what kind of common interview questions may be related to your story and think about ways you can connect the question to your strength and story. For example, the common interview question, "Can you tell me about yourself?" is usually the first question you hear in an interview. The question does not specifically ask you to share your strength. The information you would include would be more background information, education and degree history, and then you could include your strength and story that you have prepared. Immediately responding to any interview question with "my strength is..." would be awkward and come across as though you are not listening to the interviewer's questions. The key is finding a natural way to respond to common questions that do not ask you to outright share a strength and story.

Lastly, evaluate your tone, or have a friend listen in to ensure you are using a humble posture with your statements rather than a negative or prideful tone. When giving stories, some speakers can talk negatively about the other people in the scenario they are sharing. Make sure that your prepared responses simply focus on *your* strength and *your* actions. The interviewer wants to get to know about you. Do not spend valuable time talking negatively about other companies, jobs, fellow employees, or customers. In the end, this only reflects negatively on you.

What to Expect When You Are Interviewing

Do not come to an interview with the wing it mindset. It is easier to answer questions with practice and knowing those questions is not impossible. Consider using the internet to look up common interview questions. In addition to the common questions, some interviewers will ask off the wall questions like, "if you could be any kitchen appliance what would you be?" but these are questions that can still be bridged into your strength. For example, if your strength is *efficient*, you might respond, "Because I am quick, thorough, and overall efficient, I would be a toaster because they are very similar. For example ... (*then you would share your story here.*)"

After you have practiced and worked on questions, the more practical steps of preparation should be considered. First plan your attire. There are many online examples of the best clothing for an interview. Professional attire in dark or neutral tones are the best options for a professional interview. This can vary by industry and style of the business but err on the side of caution and dress your best unless you have been told otherwise from the interviewer themselves (Fig. 23.2).

Map out your travel to the interview. Plan drives or flights with enough down time between arrival and the interview. If you are interviewing locally, map out your directions the night before and, if you have the chance, practice that drive to make sure you know exactly where you need to go. Make sure you fill up your gas tank and check your air

Fig 23.2 Here you can see three strong examples of good professional interview attire. Suits and tie in calm, darker colors are always a way to catch an interviewer's eye and show you are taking the interview seriously.

Source: https://www.shutterstock.com/image-photo/two-men-one-woman-during-job-84279217

pressure in your tires to be sure your car is ready to go without any difficulty. While this may be an odd step to follow, running out of gas or having to add a stop at a gas station could throw off your schedule. Having this taken care of in advance will help you be confident the day of the interview and relieve some nerves.

Plan your day. If you have an early interview, make sure you wake up in the morning with more time than usual to get ready and have a good and healthy breakfast. You should utilize your *day of the presentation routine* to get ready. If you have an afternoon or evening time for your interview, make sure that you get to the interview location or neighborhood with plenty of time to park and review your prepared responses. Eat lunch early so you do not run behind on time. Arrive at least 15 minutes early to any appointment or interview you have with a professional organization. There may be paperwork or forms that need to be copied or completed and this allows for that to happen prior to your interview or meeting.

Bring additional copies of your resume. Find out how many people will be involved in your interview meeting and research their roles in the organization. Bring enough copies for each of them in a portfolio folder that includes a notepad. You may want to take notes during your interview so that you can ask questions at the end of the conversation. Be sure to bring identification and any other documents requested by the employer and place them in your portfolio folder (Fig. 23.3).

Research the company you are interviewing with. Knowing what they do, what their mission is, and things that you like about them that align with your personal passions will help you in forming responses to interview questions as well as being honest about why you

© By C.J. Osborne/Shutterstock.com

Fig 23.3 Consider finding a portfolio like this that has a plain cover to store your documents, additional resumes, and your pen when you attend an interview.

Source: https://www.shutterstock.com/image-vector/open-leather-business-folder-blank-notebook-56884411

would be a good fit for their organization. In addition to reviewing the company, review the job description. Consider the tasks or skills that are listed that you are most passionate about and make sure that you mention them when you discuss your strengths.

Interviews are uncomfortable. American Author Daniel Handler has considered it the equivalent to many papercuts in a day or being betrayed by family. But they do not have to be uncomfortable. If you prepare and are honest and genuine about yourself, you can walk away from an interview; regardless of the outcome, confident that you represented the best and most authentic version of yourself. Hired or not you can be happy about the opportunity to interview and see the valuable experience you have gained.

TAKE ACTION

1. List your three strengths:

   a. _____   b. _____   c. _____

2. What experience/setting did you see each strength occur?

   • _____

   • _____

   • _____

3. Summarize in a sentence or two the story about each strength in each experience

   • _____

   _____

   _____

   • _____

   _____

   _____

   • _____

   _____

   _____

4. How could you share a strength in response to some of these common interview questions:

   • Tell me about yourself
   • Tell me about a time you faced conflict in a job
   • Tell me about a time you have been asked to work in a team or group
   • Can you share a moment you saw yourself take initiative?

24 Successful Incorporation of Technology in Presentations

"Technology is best when it brings people together."

—Matt Mullenweg

By 2025, there will be 38.6 billion smart devices in use around the world. There are over 4.3 million internet users (Davis et al., 2021). In 2020, the COVID-19 pandemic led to many countries issuing stay at home orders for their citizens. This in turn led to businesses needing to adapt to a new way of working and that allowed employees to work from home. Enter technology solutions. Widespread adoption of work from home strategies created an increase of 34% in overall productivity levels. This trend will lead to a 20% reduction in brick-and-mortar business offices and lead to a more remote-style work environment for many businesses with rented office space (Davis et al., 2021). What this means is technology will be a staple tool beyond simple computer processing and it will be necessary to become skilled at using technology for presenting in order to be able to be successful in the workforce and the classroom.

Technology seems simple enough. Turn on computer, connect to the internet, start a video call or press record. However, there are elements that many people do not prioritize when using technology to deliver a presentation or participate in a class or meeting. Best practices for technological presentation aids can be found in Chapter 15. This chapter, however, will mainly focus on using technology to deliver your presentation digitally. We will review *Types of Technology*, *Video Details*, *Preparation*, and *When Technology Fails*. Knowing tools, best practices, and being prepared for anything will give you confidence when you deliver a presentation using a technology tool. So how can we go from just a regular technology user to a cool technology user?

Types of Technology

Video conferencing solutions have changed over the years. In the 2000s, many businesses used WebEx, which required a participant to watch a PowerPoint on a computer screen and listen to the presenter on a phone. Today we have online live web camera options to allow us to feel like we are all in the same room without leaving the comfort of the office or home. Two particular technological options for live presentations saw significant growth born from the necessity for working from home during the COVID pandemic. These platforms are Zoom and Microsoft Teams.

Zoom and Microsoft Teams are online interfaces that allow you to create a meeting and, with a connected video camera and microphone, join a group online, and have a meeting live. This is one of the best ways to present live. These platforms provide a connectivity among groups of people or one on one. They also offer free options so they can be used by anyone with internet access and the proper tech tools. Connections in these live meetings can be recorded and archived or shared; however, the primary use should be for live presentations (Fig. 24.1).

If your presentation is not a live meeting or event, you can consider using content creation platforms. One particular platform, Loom (www.loom.com), allows you to record yourself speaking while also sharing a screen's content, keeping your face visible through the presentation. This is an excellent tool for online courses requiring presentations, events wanting prerecorded content, or personal videos you may use for training or teaching in your profession. The best aspect for a recorded presentation is that it offers a camera view of the presenter. Nothing is more boring in a presentation than watching a slideshow with a person talking in the background. Having a face on screen helps improve engagement with audience members. Loom does require subscriptions and limits free options, so you will need to discern if it can accommodate your needs. If you do not want to invest in subscriptions or have presentations that are too long, consider using the basic tool at your fingertips – your device. Most laptops and tablets offer a front facing camera and have options for video recording. You may also use live recording options that many computers offer and even record your screen in order to show your content. This requires a higher level of computer literacy to achieve the look you want from a prerecorded

Fig 24.1 This is what a Microsoft Teams or Zoom call will look like. Notice each individual person's square. They all are professionally dressed, have decent lighting and clear video. Some could use better camera angles and lighting; however, this is a strong example of what your video presentation details should look like.

Source: https://www.shutterstock.com/image-photo/team-working-by-group-video-call-1694685136

presentation and may be too time consuming to learn. If this does not fit your needs consider the option to record using Zoom.

Regardless of your situational needs, professions all over the world are going to require a higher level of adaptability and knowledge of technology as working from home and remote jobs become more prevalent (Davis et al., 2021). This is why, even if you do not have a presentation on the calendar, you must familiarize yourself with tools that offer communication solutions that can connect you digitally to your audience.

Video Details

When professionals and students begin to work with video technology, there is often a good bit of detail that is overlooked because of limited experience using video for work or school. Presenters that simply press record and do not consider the details in the video can be seen as unprofessional resulting in detrimental results when it comes to seeking promotions, scholarships, good grades, or even jobs. That is why, if you are using a technology platform to present to an audience live or otherwise, it is necessary to consider details such as *backgrounds, microphones, clothing, camera orientation, lighting, and rehearsal.* Professor Brandon Walker, Instructor of Digital Communications at The University of West Alabama, and overall guru of video production, recommends some "pro tips" or *PROfessor Walker's tips*, to help you look like a pro at presenting with technology (2021).

Backgrounds can either enhance the presenter or fully distract the audience. Many presenters choose poor locations like dorms, outside in the unkempt back yard, in front of a glowing bright window, and all of this is because using video has not been a common practice in the workplace or in educational settings. One necessary element in a video is to set your camera up with horizontal orientation (Fig. 24.2). Think about a TV screen or a

© By New Africa/Shutterstock.com

Fig 24.2 This is a good example of how to position a mobile phone for video presentation recording or broadcasting.

Source: https://www.shutterstock.com/image-photo/female-blogger-recording-video-table-1087683914

laptop. Many people watch presentations on monitors that are set up horizontal. We have become so accustomed to using smart phones with vertical orientation, that horizontal is often ignored. This can make a video too small to see if it is shared on a horizontal platform, and also many platforms add distracting bars of blurred video on the sides to eliminate the black borders, which come up in this case. Look back at Fig. 24.1 to see some strong examples of clean backgrounds.

PROfessor Walker's Tip: choose a location with neutral and solid colors in the background such as white, tan, beige, or even light grey with minimal decoration. Additionally, the décor in the background should be professional in nature and limited on personal items (2021). Clutter, trash, and too many knick-knacks could be distracting to the audience causing them to think about what is behind you rather than what you are saying. Make sure cleanliness is visible on your screen. Pull up the camera and examine how things around you look rather than how you look and be very critical.

ABC (2020) released a television show during the summer of 2020 called *The Disney Family Sing Along.* Celebrities from all over the country filmed themselves singing beloved Disney songs from their own homes during the COVID-19 stay at home order period. One of the recurring elements that you can notice when watching each home is that when they presented in a setting that was a full room, there was very little on the counters or furniture other than basic items or Disney items. For example, Julianne Hough danced through her kitchen, and she had nothing on the counters. No toaster, coffee maker, soap dispenser, hand towels, recipe books, nothing! This made it more possible for the audience to focus on her performance and presentation rather than her home, and ultimately it was nice to see a clean undistracting space. Remove all clothes, posters, and present alone without people in the background to ensure a pleasing setting for your audience.

Background is not just about visual elements; it also includes audio elements as well. Noise in the background is distracting and completely takes away credibility of the presenter as it provides the appearance of not making an effort to create the best setting for your presentation. Find a quiet location where noise from outside is minimal. *PROfessor Walker's Tip: PLEASE, "change your smoke alarm battery and turn off your television and phone ringer/vibration!"* Hearing a loud chirping every 20–30 seconds is about as close to torture for an audience during a presentation as you can get.

Some platforms offer the opportunity to use a virtual background. Along with backgrounds, they offer filters that can turn the speaker into an animal, have bright makeup, or give them a costume. The issues with these fun additions are that they can be seen as unprofessional and look low budget. To get a realistic background that stays consistent you would need excellent lighting and a green screen to make it look professional. *PROfessor Walker's Tip: "stay away from the moving background scenes unless you are specifically going for that. No one is going to think you are really at the beach…"* (2021). The common presenter does not have tools like a green screen or professional lighting to pull off this option. However, they do not have to with a good clean professional-looking background that they can create themselves.

In February 2021, Texas Judge Roy Ferguson shared an "important zoom tip" on Twitter after lawyer Rod Ponton joined a Zoom virtual hearing and began to present only to realize he was a talking cat in the virtual meeting. The filter was difficult to remove and ultimately, he gave up and felt it necessary to share with the judge, "I'm not a cat" (Tyco, 2021). While filters are fun for social events, it is very important to test your set-up on your technological platform prior to joining meetings so you are presenting the most professional backdrop, and, in this case, putting your best, or actual, face forward.

The overall sound quality is one of the things that can contribute the most to the gratitude or frustration of your audience. Using the built-in microphones on your device may not provide a speaker with the best quality for their video presentation. Walker recommends utilizing headphones or ear buds with built-in microphones to enhance the sound quality and make your voice clear and strong without the audience having to push the volume. ***PROfessor Walker's Tip:*** *consider investing in quality equipment. He says, "if you are speaking professionally, the investment is worth it." Consider researching lavalier mics and interface that would work best for your computer or tablet.* The key is to determine if your sound is clear and sounds like you. Testing this in advance is the best way to ensure you will have the highest quality at your disposal for your presentation.

Lighting is also an important factor when creating your setting for your video presentation. Many lights can blur a camera, put a glare in the audience's eyes, or can wash out all the color in the room. Finding a good source of light or investing in a lighting set up can ensure you have the best look for your audience. Consider videos you watch on YouTube. Look at people who demonstrate video game play or make up tutorials. They have a bright light on their faces, and you can see all the video details clearly. Now, in contrast to this, consider home videos you may make. Without strong lighting, much of the screen is dark and the presenter or person on screen is hard to see unless they are facing good lighting. This alone is distracting to an audience and if it is not pleasing to look at, they will tune you out.

Test out your lighting. Even if a room feels well lit, it may not be well lit for a video of your face. Lights above the speaker create shadows on the face. Lights behind a speaker often give them little halos or wash out half of their head making their hair look bald. ***PROfessor Walker's Tip:*** *turn off ceiling fans to avoid shadows that move while it is on. Lighting from above and in front of you using a lamp or a clip-on light will provide direct light to make you easier to see. He shares, "Your light should be brighter than what is in your background so that you stand out."* Do not leave your audience in the dark, it will make them simply want to turn you off.

Now that you have your camera, background, lighting, and noise addressed, what about you? You are the main character in this video presentation, so, enter wardrobe and make up! Ok, not everyone needs make up, but clothing and appearance are necessary to consider when delivering a video presentation. Professional clothing from head to toe, clean and groomed hair, brushed teeth all signal that you take your presentation serious, even if you are sitting at home.

Clothing should be simple professional with solid cool colors. Bright colors can translate different across devices and cool colors will be more muted and not distract the audience. ***PROfessor Walker's Tip:*** *limit the use of patterns. Smaller patterns like plaid or houndstooth* (Roll Tide) *can often create a rolling or strobing effect on screen with some cameras, so be safer than sorry and limit yourself to light pinstripes or bigger patterns that are simple.* Avoid tee shirts, hooded sweatshirts, undershirts, and tank tops. Evaluate if your clothing is modest and is not as interesting as your presentation. Having a higher neckline, solid fabric, or a top without buttons can eliminate fears you may have of the audience seeing down your shirt. Again, you want them to be interested in you, not your clothes (or lack thereof).

Why head to toe professional dress? Because you never know when you might have to stand up. Tammy White, Career Services Director for The University of West Alabama, shared that in her Fall 2020 virtual career fair with employers, one employer asked the students interviewing to stand up to show they fully dressed for the occasion on a Zoom Interview. Fully dressed signals to an audience member, interviewer, employer, or even professor that you are fully committed to their meeting and ultimately their mission or work when you fully dress for success.

Eye contact can be hard to prioritize if you have a screen in front of you filled with notes. Reading your notes word for word is never recommended and is more obvious as people are seeing you even more clearly right on their screen. If you are not using notes on the screen, there is also a temptation to look at yourself to check your appearance. This can be very distracting not only to the audience, but you could lose track of what you are saying as you begin to critique how you look rather than focus on delivering great content. **PROfessor Walker's Tip:** *place a sticker or sticky note next to the camera that says "smile!" or "look here!" so that you are reminded to make eye contact with the camera and thus with the audience out there online.*

When filming yourself, it is easy to just prop a camera up or sit in front of a laptop to record. However, this can create problematic angles. Often an inexperienced video presenter will have the angle aiming right up their noses and it is not very flattering. The best practice is to find a shelf or a way to prop your camera up at slightly above eye level. The best angle is from above rather than below and will help you not only look professional, but your mother will be happy that you are sitting up straight for once.

PROfessor Walker's Tip: *"Adding technology makes it more difficult, so you should plan on practicing more." Walker recommends doubling your normal presentation rehearsal.* If you rehearse seven times as recommended in Chapter 18, Preparing for a Speech, then adding video presentation to the requirements should push you to practice 14 or more times. When Katie Burrall graduated with her Master of Arts in Integrated Marketing Communications from The University of West Alabama, she was scheduled for a job interview via Zoom prior to graduation. She planned her answers using techniques taught in Chapter 23, and then had a friend join a mock zoom call using the technology. She rehearsed in the exact location she would complete the interview, wearing her interview outfit, with the background, device, audio, and lighting she would use and went through practice questions online and shared her screen using the examples she planned to use on interview day. This allowed her to gain feedback not only on her interview question responses but also was able to evaluate volume, eye contact, camera angle, clothing, and background. This proved important as the adjustments made for a better presentation and ultimately, she was hired.

Preparation

The best way to approach technology is to never trust it to be fail or fool proof – *looking at you router and printer.* With video presentations there is a lot of checking, testing, and ultimately evaluation that must go into each of the many components that we have discussed. Much of this can occur in the day before; however, on the day of the presentation it is always good to double check some important elements to ensure you are fully prepared to present without common glitches.

The first thing on the list is to know your platform and its capabilities and how to use them to make adjustments. You can also make sure you have the information needed to access the presentation site and test that it is working. Many platforms have test features, including Zoom and Microsoft Teams, so presenters can adjust things in advance and be confident the platform has the correct settings in place. Using test rooms on these platforms should be more than just looking at the basics of audio, video, and background. This is an opportunity to fully run through your presentation. Record yourself and watch back for problems or errors. Test out visual aids you plan to share on the screen. If you are not educated on your platform, it will make you look unprepared and unpolished on presentation day.

Consider all components needed for your online and offline technology tools. First, consider your hardware: computers, hard drives, mouse, or remote. Do these require cables or batteries? If so, **PROfessor Walker's Tip:** *have a backup cable and batteries for everything that requires them. And, if a component needs charging like a laptop or a removable battery, get those charged the day before.* If you rely on your computer to be plugged in and find that the power is out to the room outlets, you will be sorry that your computer is not charged and ready. Another **PROfessor Walker's Tip:** *update software and firmware on all your devices used for the presentation. Update to the most recent application for your platform. Make sure your computer or device's operating system is at the most current version.*

Preparation must happen early and often. Some of these steps must happen during the weeks and days before, much like the preparation discussed in Chapter 18, the overall goal is to be confident in the efforts made to prepare your technological elements so you can fully focus on a presentation the day it occurs.

Technology Fails

In person and online, technology can fail, and preparing for the worst-case scenarios in advance will boost your confidence. As it was shared earlier, trust should not be placed in any technological tool. You should always have backups and that includes in person presentations. Presentation aids such as slideshows, PDF documents, and videos should be saved in multiple locations. Consider using a cloud service such as Dropbox and Google Drive, having the item on a flash drive, and having a saved file on your computer.

During rehearsal on the day before, refresh your memory on how to adjust issues with microphones and video settings on your platforms. If something cuts out or fails, you should be able to adjust more quickly when you have reviewed the steps to follow. Also have all backup presentation aids open and available at a click in the event your primary method does not work.

One core component to digitally presenting in a live setting is quality Internet service. If you have not invested in quality Internet service, you should have an alternate location to utilize – a college campus, your office, your home, or a library that provides internet so that you may connect and have confidence in your connection. You may have strong Internet; however, it is a best practice to refresh your Internet the day of your presentation to ensure it has a strong connection. **PROfessor Walker's Tip:** *before presenting reset your Internet by unplugging your modem or router for 30 seconds and then plugging it back in.*

He recommends running an Internet speed test on www.speedtest.net prior to resetting the internet and then checking it a second time once the internet has restored. This gives an accurate understanding of how strong your connection is, and you can feel confident that it is reliable or make adjustments if needed.

Technology, based on the research, is here to stay in the classroom and workplace for the foreseeable future in new ways that are stretching its users. Now it is a powerful tool for communication that goes beyond simple social media connection. It can create relationships that never would have been created as it can connect people from all over the globe, country, and community when it previously would have been impossible. The factor that will qualify technology users in the workforce and classroom is the adaptability to available tools and the willingness to become knowledgeable about those tools. The factor that will set apart users is the passion for a quality presentation beyond content when using technology. Attention to detail and creating the most professional looking video presentation can take a *good* presentation to *great* or even *amazing*. In full disclosure, having quality production (aka clean and professional details) in your video presentation could take a *really bad* presentation to *ok* or *decent* for the audience just by looking put together and clean! Don't be a regular technology user, be a cool technology user.

References

Davis, Morris, Andra Ghent, and Jesse Gregory. "The Work-from-Home Technology Boon." VOX, CEPR Policy Portal, April 18, 2021. https://voxeu.org/article/work-home-technology-boon.

Galov , Nick. "How Fast Is Technology Growing - Moore's Law Can't Keep Up." HostingTribunal, January 15, 2021. https://hostingtribunal.com/blog/how-fast-is-technology-growing/#gref.

Gilliland, Amanda. Pro tips for Video Presentations with Brandon Walker. Personal, May 25, 2021.

Gilliland, Amanda. Tips for Virtual Interviews with Tammy White. Personal, January 27, 2021.

Steinberg, Mason, and Brian Strickland. Broadcast. *The Disney Family Sing Along.* ABC, April 16, 2021.

Tyko, Kelly. "Zoom Filters Gone Wrong: Lawyer Tells Judge 'I'm Not a Cat' during Kitten Filter Mishap." USA Today. Gannett Satellite Information Network, February 11, 2021. https://www.usatoday.com/story/tech/2021/02/09/zoom-filter-warning-lawyer-cat-kitten-filter-virtual-hearing/4456097001/.

CPSIA information can be obtained
at www.ICGtesting.com
Printed in the USA
LVHW011347220822
726438LV00006B/13